St. Louis Community College

Library

5801 Wilson Avenue
St. Louis, Missouri 63110

Jerry Baker's
Fabulous Everything, Everywhere, Indoor, Outdoor Garden Answer Book

Jerry Baker's
Fabulous Everything, Everywhere, Indoor, Outdoor Garden Answer Book

by Jerry Baker

Grosset & Dunlap
A Filmways Company
Publishers • New York

To my wife, Ilene, the woman who asks the toughest questions

contents

lawn care

I have concluded from my mail that most of you would like to have your home sitting in the middle of the lawn at Mount Vernon, but you want to maintain it with a magic wand. You are looking for magic motions, potions, or lotions, and I keep telling you there is only one of those, if you want a fairly respectable lawn —and that is Elbow Grease.

If we concerned ourselves with properly spending common sense instead of improperly spending dollars and cents, we would end up with a "super-duper" lawn and save time, money, and effort.

To begin with, all lawns must be fed more than once a year if they are to be halfway presentable. Notice I didn't say you should *buy* more than once a year. I said *feed* more, so let's spend a little common

9

sense and save some copper cents. If you can afford to buy only one bag of lawn food a year, do yourself and your lawn a favor. Don't let the lawn eat it all at once. 'Cause that lawn food is just going to go to waste. Set your lawn spreader at low and feed early in the spring, feed again in early summer, again in early fall, and whatever is left over give to your lawn as a nightcap. Now, to make the lawn food really work, water your lawn right after you feed it, with one ounce of liquid soap to fifteen gallons of water over 2,500 square feet, and watch that lawn turn into the jewel of the neighborhood.

OK, big spender (common sense, that is)! Let's go to the mower shop and buy two used, sharp mower blades. Now, mow that grass every time it grows one-half inch, and each time you do so, mow it in a different direction. Change the blade every fifth cut and sharpen the blade you take off. Always pick up the clippings, and add them to your vegetable garden for weed control. Water before two o'clock in the afternoon at least three times a week with the lawn sprinkler that makes a lot of noise so you know it's not lying down on the job. I like all sprinklers, but the pulsator is my favorite.

If you have the kind of lawn that you dream of, you are bound to have a visitor or two. No, I am not talking about your brother-in-law. However, this visitor has about the same size appetite. Insects—any one of twenty-three of the most common varieties. Don't panic! Remember, we are only spending common

10

sense. If you will continue the soap-and-water shower at least every three weeks and add an ounce of tobacco juice to the fifteen gallons of water, any bug that stops by to freeload will be so sick he won't come back. If one does persist, let him have it with the least expensive, most effective medication recommended. The tobacco formula is one-half plug or pouch of chewing tobacco in one quart of hot water and save it for use through the season. The mixture can also be used in flower and vegetable gardens, and on trees, shrubs, and evergreens.

Lawn diseases should not be a problem if you are on the common-sense spending spree I have recommended. Just as soap and water kill bacteria on us, they do so on your lawn and plants. If an odd spot or patch shows up, look for dog damage, children damage, gas damage; then go for medical (plant, that is) help.

Recently, questions have been raised about the safety of Chlordane. I have always found it to be effective and safe and I will continue to use it. However, if you are concerned you can use Diazinon as an alternative.

Q. *When is the best time to plant grass seed?*

A. Between August 15 and September 20, when the days are warm and the evenings are cool. The first day of spring by Mother Nature's calendar begins August 15. Grass seed can be planted at any time if it

11

is kept damp and fed lightly with a liquid plant food. (I use my house-plant food, believe it or not, in a hose gun sprayer.)

Q. *What can you do to make grass seed sprout faster?*

A. Scare the hell out of it. You can also add one cup of weak tea (orange, green, or black) to each pound of seed and place it in the refrigerator for 3 to 5 days. Remove from the refrigerator and spread out on the driveway, basement, or garage floor to dry slightly so that you can handle it, then plant. This method should make sprouting time five to six times faster.

Q. *Is there any difference between cheap grass seed and expensive?*

A. The price, to begin with. Grass seed is a commodity bought, sold, and traded like any other grain and seed. Futures are bought and sold with prices being decided on the basis of availability, which is determined by weather. Good weather produces a good quality, large crop, which generally results in lower prices; bad weather produces smaller quantities for which there is big demand, which forces prices up. If anyone asks you whether you deal in commodities, and if you own a lawn, you can seriously say yes —grass seed.

12

Q. I have seed left over from last year. Is it still good?

A. As a rule, yes, but to find out for sure, fill a paper, plastic, or styrofoam cup three-quarters full of water and add a used tea bag for a minute or two. Then sprinkle a teaspoonful of seed on top of the water; set in a well-lighted window. In a couple of weeks you should see grass. The tea-and-refrigeration method will improve marginal seed performance.

Q. What can you do to keep the birds off new grass seed until it sprouts?

A. Adopt six or seven cats. Cover the seed with ¼ inch of topsoil, pat down or roll gently. The faster it sprouts, the more you keep and the less the birds eat. You can also slit an old tennis ball and force it over the end of a 6- to 7-foot piece of old garden hose. Draw two mean eyes and a nasty mouth, as well as placing yellow strips of tape like Xs down the hose. Let this lie on the seeded area until the seed sprouts. Why? The birds think it's a snake. Only eagles and hawks won't be fooled, but then they don't eat seed.

Q. Which blend of grass seed is best for a play area?

A. Plastic, concrete, and iron, none of which is available yet. In the South you can count on U-3 Bermuda grass, and in the North Kentucky 31 tall fescue. I want to caution anyone who is planting a play area not to be tempted to add clover seed to these areas to fill in

13

spots as it can cause injuries. Clover is slippery, and when running feet try to stop quickly, clover won't cooperate.

Q. Which grass seed is best for a shady spot?

A. None, really. That's not exactly true, but then they haven't developed an astro-turf seed yet. There is no true shade grass; all grasses like some sun. However, the best of the bunch that get along with less sun than the rest is Poa Trivialis. Kentucky 31 tall fescue, *Zoysia Japonica, Zoysia Matrella,* Astoria bent, Highland and Pencross bents, as well as creeping red, Illahee, and Chewings fescue all will tolerate a light shade.

Q. Which grass seed do you recommend for a really steep embankment?

A. As a rule, none. It's not that many grasses won't grow and hold on hillsides; it's your safety I am concerned with. More accidents occur from falls and severe cuts from mowers on hillside maintenance. I would prefer that for your own safety you plant any of the low- or no-maintenance ground covers.

Q. What's the toughest grass seed you can think of for a family of five boys and three dogs?

A. Inverted wire brushes set in concrete and painted green. For something softer, you can depend on

14

Kentucky 31 or Alta, Goars, or Meadow coarse fescue.

Q. Can I grow a bent-grass lawn from seed or must I use plugs?

A. Positively and without a doubt you can grow it from seed. Be my guest. Astoria, Highland, Penncross, or Seaside bents all can be grown from sown seed. Before tackling a bent lawn, though, make sure you understand that they take a ton of work.

Q. What's the difference between all the different rye grasses?

A. What do you mean all? There is perennial or annual. If you are talking about brand names, they are improved varieties of the same two. I have found NK-100 to be about the best of the lot.

Q. It may sound funny, but can I have a different-type front lawn, back yard, retreat area, and putting green all at one home?

A. Sure, why not. Just remember—sex knows no barrier, and if clippings or seed are transferred from location to location, there is going to be some hanky-panky, with the possibility of a strange lawn born out of wedlock.

15

Q. *How often do you water new seed?*

A. Enough to keep it damp (moist), so that depends on where you live and when you plant. Remember, I said damp, not soggy wet.

Q. *When do you feed a new lawn?*

A. Before you plant. With a cheap lawn food, set on the lowest spreader setting and till into the soil when you prepare for seed. I feed with a weak liquid solution of lawn or plant food—just enough to change the color of the water in the base sprinkler jar.

Q. *Can you sow grass seed in the winter?*

A. Why not? Remember, just before a snow, top-dress with a light sprinkle of soil (topdressing is a blanket of soil) so the birds don't think you are a horticultural philanthropist.

Q. *Why do they dye grass seed with different colors?*

A. Some companies do it for the fun of it, as a sales gimmick; others coat the seed with an insecticide or fungicide. Read the bag. It will tell you if they are kidding or serious.

Q. *Should you add grass seed to an old lawn every year?*

16

A. Only if you are too darn lazy the rest of the year to feed, de-thatch, water, and mow it properly.

Q. *Can you plant grass seed where a dog killed the grass or grass died over the winter?*

A. Yep! Scratch up the dead grass, say a prayer, soak and refrigerate the new seed, scatter and top-dress lightly, pat or tamp down and—voila! New grass!

Q. *If grass seed freezes in the garage over the winter, is it still good?*

A. Hell, yeh! If it goes to seed in the wild, do you think it builds a new house to keep warm in in the winter? It just goes dormant (to sleep); it will wake up in time to give you a good lawn.

Q. *How many different kinds of grass seed are there?*

A. How many stars are there in the sky, raindrops in a cloud, grains of sand on a beach? Every time I turn around they have a new "strain." For all intents and purposes, there are 30 to 35 popular types of lawn grass seed.

Q. *We moved from the East Coast to the Southwest.*

Everyone gives us a different recommendation as to types of lawn. Who really knows?

A. Your feet or a bicycle. Take a walk in your new neighborhood. Look at lawns—different kinds, the ones that are well kept. Stop and introduce yourself and ask questions—how much time, effort, and money was spent—and then make up your own mind.

Q. Some grass seed is for shade, some is for wet areas, some for sand, and so on. Give us a simple description of which is which.

A. You have got to be kidding. It would be here from now till harvest. All grasses like sunny, well-drained locations. The fescues will tolerate some shade, which means a little dampness. If you feed properly—water clay shorter but often, sand long and deep, and good soil three times a week—you can't miss.

Q. We had some grass seed that had sprouted in the bag. My wife threw it out. She said it wouldn't grow. Was she right?

A. She was sort of right. In most cases, it would have had marginal growth, but it would have rooted. It's best to start with fresh seed.

Q. I have heard that grass seed in plastic bags is not

18

as good as grass seed in cloth or paper bags. Is this true?

A. It would depend on whether you are selling cloth or plastic bags. It doesn't make a bit of difference as far as I'm concerned.

Q. Do the numbers and dates on bags of seed mean anything, or do they just make them up?

A. Certainly they mean something. The purity percent indicates what percent of the seed in the bag is the seed variety you are purchasing. Germination figures tell you the results of a sprout test the land-grant college performed for the state in which the seed was grown. The weed content tells you what percent of weeds you can expect.

Q. What's the best type of grass seed to grow for animals' play area?

A. Either of the tall fescues, Kentucky 31 or Meadow.

Q. Is it true that grass seed cannot be planted in hot, dry weather?

A. No, it is not true. If you will soak, refrigerate, scratch up the soil, top-dress, pat down, and keep damp, it will sprout at any time.

Q. Should we cover up our grass seed with straw?

19

A. Your neighbors will hate you, but you can if you want. Why not just top-dress, roll with a near-empty roller, and keep the neighbors happy?

Q. *Can you plant new seed if you have used a crab-grass killer?*

A. If you have used a crabgrass killer—that is, one which kills the mature plant—you can go ahead and plant seed with no problem. But if you have used a pre-merge, which is used in early spring to kill dormant seed, forget it.

Q. *How old does new grass have to be before you can use weed and feed?*

A. I like it to have undergone at least three mowings and one good, normal feeding.

Q. *How tall should new grass be before you mow it?*

A. Tall enough to go through the mower set at 1½ inches for most cool grasses. But with bent grass, you should let it get its feet in the ground a couple of weeks before you mow.

Q. *What's the best type of lawn to grow on clay soil?*

A. If you can get that soil loose enough by using Grand Prize Lawn and Garden Gypsum 50 pounds per 1,000 square feet, then any grass seed will grow.

20

Q. Is there a right time of the day to plant seed?

A. I always try to plant, drill, or broadcast seed after five P.M. Plants grow in the dark so I give them a head start.

Q. Should you spread seed by hand or can you use your lawn spreader?

A. I find that you get better coverage by using a cyclone-type broadcast spreader. If you don't own one, borrow one. The next spreader you purchase should be this type.

Q. How deep should you plant grass seed?

A. Big seed like rye, ½ inch; medium like fescue, ¼ inch; and fine like merion, ⅛ to ¼ inch.

Q. Do you really have to hire those expensive companies to plow up and grind your dirt in order to have a nice lawn?

A. Only if you are lazy or rich. Pick up all wood, stones, glass, brick, rocks, or other debris, and go rent a roto-tiller. It's a great way to lose weight and does a hell of a job.

Q. Can I have a zoysia lawn in Wisconsin?

A. Sure, you can, but I don't know why you would

want to. It's the first to turn brown in the fall when the temperature gets into the 40s and the last to turn green in the spring—unless you want to dye it.

Q. How far apart do you plant plugs of grass?

A. I guess it depends on how long you want to wait for your lawn to fill in. For folks with patience, 8 to 10 inches will do, and for those with ants in their pants, 3 to 5 inches apart.

Q. When is the best time to plant stolons of grass?

A. In the spring, the first day of which is August 15. That's Mother Nature's spring. September 20 is probably the best, and you can go three days on either side.

Q. What is the difference between stolons, plugs, and sprigs?

A. Stolons are lengths of grass roots with some foliage attached; plugs are coin-sized and -shaped pieces of grass; and sprigs are pieces of root with a piece of foliage.

Q. When do you feed new lawns planted by stolons?

A. I wait 5 days and then lightly feed with any liquid plant, lawn, or garden food at 25 percent of the recommended rate.

22

Q. How do I stop weeds from growing between my plugs of bent lawn before it fills in?

A. Not for 6 to 8 weeks, and then make darn sure the weed killer you use definitely says "safe near bent."

Q. Is sod better than seed?

A. Only if you are short on patience and long on money. No matter how you cut it, you have to wait for the seed to sprout, and sod is instant.

Q. When is the best time to sod?

A. Whenever you have the money and the man's got the sod. Early spring and mid-fall are probably the safest time to avoid the grass burning up from lack of watering.

Q. How soon after you sod do you feed?

A. I wait until the second time I cut it and then feed with a lightweight nonburning or liquid feed.

Q. Can you water sod too much?

A. Not as a rule the first week. I have found that if you pay extra attention around the edges (walks, drives, and curbs), a once-a-day soaking will do fine.

Q. My new sod has what looks like eyes (brown) on

23

the blades. I noticed it the day after it was laid. Is it sick?

A. You bet your grass it's sick. The ailment is called leaf spot. The chemical cure is Acti-Dine or Fore, but you shouldn't have to pay for treatment. Call the crook that sold you that pig-in-a-poke and make him take care of it.

Q. How short do you mow new sod?

A. I keep it at 1½ inches on merion and Kentucky blue. Mow as soon as the grass shows a growth of 2 inches, and collect the clippings.

Q. How long do I have to leave the wooden stakes in the sod on the side of a hill?

A. Until you are sure the new roots have a good grip on the soil. Grab a handful of grass the same way your teacher grabbed your hair when you were a kid, and *gently* tug. If it holds, remove the stakes. Should any slide appear, replace the stakes; if you forget, your lawn mower will let you know.

Q. How many different types of lawn can be planted by sod?

A. All of the blues, bent, fescue, and Timothy rye. I have honestly seen darn near every domestic type of lawn grass applied as sod.

24

Q. Can I use weed killer to kill the weeds growing between my sod?

A. You can, but I would caution you to wait until the third mowing and then a week after the first feeding. Let the grass recover from the shock of transplanting before you give it a dose of foul-tasting medicine.

Q. Should I leave the grass clippings on new sod?

A. How would you like the barber or hairdresser dousing your head with glue and then dropping all the hair clippings back on your head?

Q. Shouldn't you roll new sod?

A. With a very light roller; just enough to let the roots make a solid contact with the soil.

Q. I cannot afford to sod my whole lawn. Can I seed the other half and ever have it look as good as the sodded half?

A. Sure, you can. It all started from seed. If you seed in early fall you will see results sooner. Jack Barber, my next-door neighbor, did it your way. He made only one mistake; he didn't use the same variety and you can see the difference, though it doesn't look bad. If you have the same problem as Jack, overseed lightly with the same variety seed in the fall; top-dress the mixed grass with a light sprinkle of soil, blending the two into each other.

25

Q. Our merion blue sod is two weeks old, and the blades next to the house and buildings are all covered with white dust. What's wrong?

A. You bought your sod from the same crook the guy with the brown spots did! (I'm just kidding.) The powder is mildew caused by lack of sunshine and grass that's too long. Cut more often, and feed less in those spots.

Q. We had our lawn sodded three months ago, and I can still pull it up. It grew, but when we try to mow it, it lifts. How can we make roots?

A. See if your garden center has a bag or two of 0–20–20 or a low-nitrogen garden food.

Q. What's the best formula fertilizer for a bluegrass sod lawn?

A. Whichever one you can afford. Your grass doesn't care, 'cause it can't read. I apply two normal feedings, one in the spring and one in the fall. Feed after two or three mowings, with any "cyclone" spreader set on #1. Wow, what a lawn!

Q. How do you figure how many rolls of sod you need for any given area?

A. Length times width divided by nine will tell you how many rolls of sod you will need for that given

26

area. Make sure you deduct house, garage, and flower beds.

Q. Why would anyone want to sow grass seed over newly laid sod?

A. I don't know! You tell me. First, it's a waste of good money, and second, you are asking for trouble because there are unwanted grasses and weed seed in the bag.

Q. Should you apply a lawn fungicide to sod laid in the summer?

A. Only if the sod gets sick. And then, as they say in the military: Move it! Move it! Move it! Move what? It rhymes with grass.

Q. What is Hydro seeding and is it recommended for homeowners?

A. It is a method of seeding by mixing the seed into a foamy plastic-type material and applying it with a high-pressure hose. Would I recommend it to homeowners? I guess not; I have yet to see a good full-stand Hydro-seed job.

Q. My husband wants to sow grass seed himself, and then have our lot Hydro seeded on top of that. The seed underneath will be wasted, won't it?

27

A. No, as a matter of fact, that's probably going to be the seed that will sprout, and the Hydro foam and a little seed would protect it. You can save some money, though, by just seeding.

Q. *Can any seed be used in Hydro seeding?*

A. Sure, it can; all with about the same degree of success.

Q. *Don't you have to water a lawn when it is Hydro seeded?*

A. Yep! Just like any other seed job. Keep it damp.

Q. *When do you feed a Hydro-seeded lawn?*

A. After the first time you cut it.

Q. *We live in an area that has what looks like gravel. Water runs right through it. Can we possibly have a lawn?*

A. Sure, you can; you will just have to water a lot more often.

Q. *What can you add to sand to make it hold water?*

A. Clay, sawdust, or peat moss. Take a plastic gallon jug or two and poke holes in the bottom, fill with sand, and pour water over it. See how long it takes

28

from the time you pour until it comes out the bottom. Now, add the material until you lengthen the time to four times.

Q. I have a lawn full of weeds. When is the best time to kill them and with what?

A. The best time is when they are growing their best, both spring and fall. Use the safest, most effective, and cheapest weed killer you can buy.

Q. Won't weed killers hurt birds and pets?

A. Sure, if you feed it to them. Keep the pets off for at least a day. The birds don't like the smell and generally stay away for two or three days.

Q. Is it better to use liquid weed killer or dry?

A. When it is properly applied with a compression sprayer (tank type), I will go with liquid any time. But if you don't want to take the time, use dry.

Q. When is the best time of the day to apply weed killer?

A. Between 11 A.M. and 3 P.M. because the dew dampness helps carry the chemical to the roots and when it is hot and dry they drink without thinking and ZAP.

29

Q. Is it really necessary to use so many different kinds of weed killers?

A. I'm afraid so, because, like people, weeds all come in different sizes, shapes, and forms.

Q. Should you mow your lawn before applying a weed killer?

A. I don't! I wait at least three days. Remember, the good guys smell and taste the weed killer too, and it gives them an upset stomach. So, wait a day or so to cut their hair.

Q. When is the best time to kill crabgrass?

A. Before it is crabgrass! That's when it is still seed. You might call it performing a horticultural abortion. In early spring (March or April), apply a pre-merge crabgrass control.

Q. Is it better to treat only the weed areas and not the whole lawn?

A. I will go along with that and add only that you give a 10 percent fringe factor (go 10 percent beyond).

Q. Should you water right after you apply weed killers?

A. Please read the directions on the bag, bottle, or can. Do what you are told.

30

Q. If all the weeds don't die, can I spray again?

A. Take a weed that lived through the battle to your garden center to make sure that the weed killer you have will do the job on this type of weed.

Q. What do you use to clean out your sprayers?

A. Soap, water, and baking soda.

Q. What's the easiest way to tell if spots in your lawn are caused by insects, disease, animals, or fertilizer and chemicals?

A. Take the spot to your neighborhood garden spot checker (garden center).

Q. Is there a guaranteed way to spray lawn insects and be sure that they are killed?

A. If you spray the right time, the right way, and with the right thing, you can be certain—but since neither you nor I can ever control all those variables, the answer is no!

Q. What's the best nonpoisonous spray to use on a lawn?

A. To do what? You try to use the mildest medication to control any illness and then work up to a stronger medication.

31

Q. *When is the best time of the day to spray your lawn for insects?*

A. Late in the afternoon or early evening, just before the "dew" comes.

Q. *Is there a sure cure for chinch bugs?*

A. I have found that a spring and fall application of Grand Prize Lawn and Garden Gypsum really does the job. The chemicals most commonly used are Dursban or Sevin.

Q. *Our baby is eaten alive by chiggers. What can we use to kill the bugs but be safe with the baby?*

A. Safety first! *Keep the baby out of the sprayed area for at least 24 hours* to ease the minds of the environmentalists and then spray the room with Malathion, which I consider mild, safe, and effective around people, pets, and plants.

Q. *How do you get rid of slugs in your lawn?*

A. For those of you who are surprised to see this question in the lawn area, don't be. Slugs and their shelled cousins from France do feed on grass. They are also not an insect, and to finally answer the question, a medication called Zectran does the job on turf areas.

32

Q. Where do earwigs come from?

A. From heaven like the rest of God's creations. The earwig is in both the good and the bad bug families, but his bads outdo his goods, so we must remove his presence. The good is that he eats some smaller insects; the bad is that he eats everything else in sight—food stuff, house plants, and flowers. He sleeps all day and eats all night, hides indoors in dark places and outside in dark, dry places. To keep him outside, spray or dust around your house foundation with Dursban or Sevin and spray plants with Malathion.

Q. Sod webworms are carrying off our lawn. How do we stop them?

A. Punch many holes in the soil area where the damage has occurred and 10 percent beyond. Now water the lawn with one ounce of your liquid soap per gallon and then spray Chlordane, Diazinon, Sevin, or Dursban.

Q. Do mosquitoes live in grass? And how do you get rid of them?

A. They sure do live in the grass, and in all other cool, damp places. Mosquitoes can be controlled in your own area by spraying shrubs, grass, gutters, under lawn furniture, and wet spots with DiBrome and Chlordane or Diazinon.

33

Q. *We have sprayed the lawn with everything to get rid of clover mites. They come into the house and cover the walls. What kills them?*

A. Clover mites won't bite you or your kids, so that worry is gone. In the house vacuum them and spray with a house bomb or use a pest strip. Outside use Malathion, Chlordane, Diazinon, or Kelthane.

Q. *We have small dogs that are being driven nuts by ticks. What can we use to be safe around the dogs?*

A. To begin with, dust the dog with the proper medication recommended by your *vet.* If the dog runs near shrubs and small-tree areas, spray those areas with Sevin, Chlordane, Diazinon, or Malathion.

Q. *I would sure like to get rid of the ants that fly, crawl, and march around my yard and garden, but if I stop them in one place they show up in another. Is there a way?*

A. Rent a roller with an attachment that has small spikes for making holes. Now add only enough weight to just make the points go into the ground. Water the lawn with one ounce liquid soap per gallon per 2,500 square feet and follow up with Chlordane or Diazinon.

Q. *My grass gets more diseases than my kids did. Where do they come from and how do you get rid of them?*

A. Plant diseases travel just like people diseases do—by hand, air, foot, and dirty tools. To cure, use plant fungicides. I find that a lawn fungicide called Fore at 8 ounces per 1,000 square feet of lawn does the job. That's usually mixed in 5 to 7 gallons of water.

Q. If you have both insects and lawn diseases, can you treat both of them at once?

A. Sure, you can. That's like saying you can't treat athlete's food and a sore throat at the same time. To make sure that both garden medications work, punch many little holes in the infected areas, water, then apply one ounce of liquid soap to 15 gallons of water over the same area. Then apply the insect control, next the disease control, or wait 3 to 5 days in between.

Q. What can we do to stop the grass from dying where our dog wets?

A. Apply garden gypsum at 50 pounds per 2,500 square feet in the fall and early spring.

Q. Is it true that moles come in your yard only if you have grubs in the lawn?

A. And skunks, too. The animals are really doing you a favor, because they are alerting you to a problem. The two best garden chemicals to control lawn insects are Zectran and Chlordane or Diazinon.

35

Q. My son and his friends wash their cars in our drive and use soap. Won't this kill our lawn and trees?

A. Heck, no! This will make them grow better. I wash my garden and lawn once a month with one ounce of liquid soap to 15 gallons of water whether they need it or not.

Q. My husband changed the oil in our car and accidentally spilled almost all of it on the lawn. The grass is dead, and I was told nothing would ever grow there again. Could this be true?

A. No, this could not be true. Try to remove 8 to 10 inches of soil and replace. Spread garden gypsum at 50 pounds per 1,000 square feet of oil spillage.

Q. I have a business office on a busy main street. All winter rock salt is scattered from county trucks. It kills my lawn and shrubs. Is there anything to take care of this?

A. Gypsum wins again. Fifty pounds per 1,000 square feet in the fall and 50 pounds per 2,500 square feet in the spring.

Q. Is green moss a disease?

A. No, it's plant life that grows in the shade where it is cool, dark, and damp. If you have a moss problem, change these conditions.

36

Q. How do you get rid of fairy ring?

A. Kill the sandman. (I'm just fooling.) Use the fungicide Fore at fourteen-day intervals.

Q. How often should you feed bent grass?

A. I feed in the spring, summer, and fall with Milorganite sludge-base lawn food.

Q. Are merion blue and Kentucky blue lawns fed the same way and with the same food?

A. They sure are. After all, they are brothers. Feed in the spring and fall as recommended by the manufacturer, and then every third cutting. Set your lawn spreader on the lowest setting, and feed with any lawn food.

Q. I have a mixed-seed back lawn, Kentucky blue, red fescue, rye, and tall fescue, while my front lawn is merion blue. I feed the back just as often as the front, but it looks worse. What's wrong?

A. Fescue grasses do not like a lot of food. One feeding in the spring should do fine.

Q. How do you know how much lawn food you need for your lawn?

A. Multiply the length of your property by the width

37

and divide by ten. Then divide that answer by the nitrogen figure on any fertilizer bag or box. The end result will tell you exactly how many pounds you must buy of the stuff you are looking at. $L \times W \div 10 \div N =$ your purchase.

$$\begin{array}{c} 200' \\ 100' \end{array} \qquad = 20,000 \text{ sq. ft.}$$

$$10\overline{\smash{\big)}20{,}000}^{\,2{,}000} \quad = 20\overline{\smash{\big)}2{,}000}^{\,100}$$

Lawn
20–10–5
Food

You would need to buy 100 pounds of this lawn food.

Q. Is it good to use a different type of lawn food in the spring, summer, and fall?

A. I do, and my golf course and sod growers do, regularly—lawn food in the spring, Milorganite in the summer, and garden food in the fall.

Q. Is there something you can put on your grass to keep it from growing?

A. Science Products has a super material called Stop Grass which slows the grass down to nothing and is used for borders.

Q. Is liquid lawn food as good as dry?

A. If you can afford it, I think it's great. I use both from time to time so my lawn doesn't get bored.

Q. How do you know when your lawn needs lime?

A. Take a soil test with a piece of litmus paper. Get it in a drugstore or at your garden center.

Q. Is there a thing called liquid lime?

A. Yep, sure is. One gallon is equal to 500 pounds of the dry, dusty, messy stuff. I use it, and I'm pleased with the results.

Q. My sister says she uses liquid gypsum. I didn't know it would dissolve. Does it?

A. She probably uses a material called "liquid-like gypsum." It's not gypsum. It does break up clay soil, but does not contain all the things gypsum does and will not repair salt damage. This material isn't bad; as a matter of fact, not bad at all. Oh! It contains enzymes.

✳ *Q. How do you discourage dogs and squirrels from digging in your lawn?*

A. I have used paradichlorobenzene moth crystals on the soil to discourage animals.

39

Q. *Is it true that only female dogs burn up shrubs and grass?*

A. That's what they say, but on occasion, when males are not given enough drinking water, they cause the same damage.

Q. *When do you de-thatch a lawn and which kinds of grasses should be de-thatched?*

A. I like to de-thatch in late fall, following up with grass seed and lawn food. Then let the snow hide the cosmetic surgery. I suggest that you de-thatch the blues and the fescues.

Q. *Should you top-dress an old lawn every year?*

A. I seldom recommend it unless you are overseeding it in spring or fall.

Q. *Will cat manure hurt my lawn?*

A. Not unless your dog catches the cat putting it there.

Q. *Is there a cure for fairy rings?*

A. If you can find someone to marry them. The chemical Fore by Science Products might help get rid of them.

40

Q. We have year-old merion blue sod that is dying from fusarium blight. What will stop it and not cost me a fortune?

A. About the best thing available right now is Benomyl or Tersan 1991, and prayer.

Q. What do skunks and moles have in common? They are both making a mess out of my yard and my social life.

A. What they both have in common is your lawn and the bugs underneath it. Kill the insects, and your social life will return.

Q. Can you get rid of weeds by burning them off on property on which you are going to plant grass seed?

A. Burning off weeds only kills the tops and the new seed, but the roots will return to haunt you again.

Q. Can I mow weeds down and sod over them and not worry?

A. That's like sweeping dirt under the rug. Someday you have got to remove it. Weeds will find their way through the cracks and take over the whole lawn.

Q. How do I get rid of crabgrass?

A. Crabgrass is best controlled before it gets a start

41

and that means destroying the seed with a pre-merge crabgrass control in early spring before the soil temperature reaches 50 degrees. If you miss this time, use a chemical called Amine Methyl Arsonate (Science Products crabgrass killer).

Q. *How do I get rid of wild garlic?*

A. 2, 4-D or Banvel-D (Velsicol).

Q. *How do I get rid of poison ivy?*

A. Carefully! And Ammate-X (Du Pont).

Q. *How do I get rid of poison oak?*

A. Just as carefully as poison ivy. And Ammate-X (Du Pont).

Q. *How do I get rid of dandelions?*

A. Before the reporters find them. 2, 4-D or Banvel-D (Velsicol).

Q. *How do I get rid of big-leafed plantain?*

A. You can use it for a tea to purge the devil. 2, 4-D or Banvel-D (Velsicol) will also wipe it out.

Q. *How do I get rid of buckhorn?*

42

A. With a shoehorn. 2, 4-D or Banvel-D (Velsicol).

Q. *How do I get rid of chickweed?*

A. Plant it in a terrarium. 2, 4-D or Banvel-D (Velsicol).

Q. *How do I get rid of henbit?*

A. 2, 4-D or Banvel-D (Velsicol).

Q. *How do I get rid of beggarweed?*

A. 2, 4-D or Banvel-D (Velsicol).

Q. *How do I get rid of clover?*

A. Rent your lawn to a dairy farmer. 2, 4-D or Banvel-D (Velsicol).

Q. *How do I get rid of pennywort?*

A. 2, 4-D or Banvel-D (Velsicol).

Q. *How do I get rid of yarrow?*

A. 2, 4-D or Banvel-D (Velsicol).

Q. *How do I get rid of sheep sorrel?*

A. 2, 4-D or Banvel-D (Velsicol).

Q. *How do I get rid of knotweed?*

A. 2, 4-D or Banvel-D (Velsicol).

Q. *How do I get rid of ground ivy?*

A. You could tell everyone you put it there on purpose. 2, 4-D or Banvel-D (Velsicol).

Q. *How do I get rid of heal all?*

A. Make a poultice. 2, 4-D or Banvel-D (Velsicol).

Q. *How do I get rid of oxalis (wood sorrel)?*

A. 2, 4-D or Banvel-D (Velsicol).

Q. *How do I get rid of quack grass?*

A. Amino Triazole.

Q. *How do I get rid of Bermuda grass?*

A. Spot-treat with Dalapon (Dow).

Q. *How do I get rid of nut grass?*

A. 2, 4-D or Banvel-D (Velsicol).

Q. *How do I get rid of creeping bent?*

A. Spot-treat with Dalapon (Dow).

44

Q. How do I get rid of tall fescue?

A. Spot-treat with Dalapon (Dow).

Q. How do I get rid of dallis grass?

A. Amine Methyl Arsonate (Science).

Q. How do I get rid of muhlenbergia?

A. Dalapon (Dow).

Q. How do I get rid of yellow fox tail?

A. Amine Methyl Arsonate (Science).

Q. How do I get rid of sand spur?

A. Spot-treat with Dalapon (Dow).

Q. How do I get rid of goose grass?

A. Amine Methyl Arsonate (Science).

Q. How do I get rid of wild violets?

A. 2, 4-D or Banvel-D (Velsicol).

Q. How do you kill sod webworms?

A. Chlordane, Diazinon, Dursban.

Q. *How do you kill white grubs?*

A. Dursban, Chlordane, Diazinon.

Q. *How do you kill Japanese beetle grubs?*

A. Chlordane, Diazinon.

Q. *How do you kill slugs?*

A. Zectran.

Q. *How do you kill millipedes?*

A. Sevin, Chlordane, Diazinon.

Q. *How do you kill centipedes?*

A. Sevin, Chlordane, Diazinon.

Q. *How do you kill snails?*

A. Zectran.

Q. *How do you kill cutworms?*

A. Sevin, Diazinon, Chlordane.

Q. *How do you kill ants?*

A. Chlordane, Diazinon, BayGon.

46

Q. *How do you kill mole crickets?*

A. Chlordane, Diazinon.

Q. *How do you kill army worms?*

A. Sevin, Chlordane, Diazinon.

Q. *How do you kill ticks?*

A. Malathion, Sevin.

Q. *How do you kill spiders?*

A. Chlordane, Diazinon.

Q. *How do you kill red clover mites?*

A. Kelthane.

Q. *How do you kill mosquitoes?*

A. Dursban, Chlordane, Diazinon.

Q. *How do you kill grass hoppers?*

A. Sevin.

Q. *How do you kill lawn moths?*

A. Sevin.

Q. How do you kill chinch bugs?

A. Dursban, Baygon, Sevin, Gypsum.

Q. How do you kill chiggers?

A. Malathion, Diazinon, Chlordane.

Q. How do you kill fiery skippers?

A. Dursban, Sevin.

Q. How do you kill leaf hoppers?

A. Malathion, Sevin, Dursban.

Q. How do you kill earwigs?

A. Chlordane, Sevin, Dursban.

Q. How do you kill pillbugs?

A. Chlordane, Diazinon.

Q. Please tell me how to get rid of dollar spot.

A. Benomyl, Fore.

Q. How do I get rid of copper spot?

A. Fore.

48

Q. *How do I get rid of rust on lawn grass?*

A. Fore.

Q. *How do I get rid of melting out?*

A. Fore.

Q. *How do I get rid of fading out?*

A. Fore.

Q. *How do I get rid of red thread?*

A. Fore.

Q. *How do I get rid of anthracnose?*

A. Maneb.

Q. *How do I get rid of brown patch?*

A. Fore.

Q. *How do I get rid of cottony blight?*

A. Benomyl, Fore.

Q. *How do I get rid of toadstools?*

A. Soap and water, Fore.

Q. How do I get rid of slime molds?

A. Fore, Benomyl.

Q. When is the best time to mow a lawn?

A. Whenever you would be comfortable, which is usually in the early evening when the heat of the day has passed. When you cut grass late in the day, dew covers the fresh cuts and soothes it before the sun comes up the next day.

Q. How short should you mow a lawn in the spring?

A. If you are talking about the blues, I drop the blade to cut just above the green that can be seen underneath. This means that my blade is usually set for 1 to 1½ inches.

Q. What's the best kind of a mower for Windsor grass?

A. A sharp one. This goes for any other type of lawn as well.

Q. Isn't a built-in sprinkler better than lawn sprinklers?

A. If you have the money, it is; if you don't, it isn't. It all

50

depends on whether you feel the convenience is worth it.

Q. When is the best time to water a lawn?

A. Before two o'clock in the afternoon. Never let a lawn go to sleep with wet hair, or the tonic you will have to buy might cost more than your lawn.

Q. Dear Sir: I am the sales manager of a large national moving company and sales representatives are constantly asking what types of lawns grow in different states and if people should leave the old lawn mower behind. Where do we get the answers?

A. Dear Mr. Sales Manager: You will do your customers a big favor if you will have a card printed up with the address of each "state land-grant college." This will also make your job easier because these colleges will send free garden and lawn information. As for the mower going on the trip, by all means, and then trade it in on a new one.

Q. What's the best kind of spreader for weed and feed?

A. It's not the spreader we worry about, it's the spreadee. You are the "spreadee." Any spreader works fine, though I prefer a cyclone (broadcast type), and I go slow and watch what I am doing.

51

Q. Are weeds killed faster with liquid or dry weed killer?

A. Liquid will generally begin faster, but they both end up doing the same job, "killing the weeds."

Q. Should you use a hose jar sprayer or a compression sprayer for weed killers?

A. I prefer using a tank-type compression sprayer because I can better control it. Remember, how you spray does make a difference.

Q. Are grass clippings good for a compost pile?

A. They sure are. Just make sure that you spread a thin layer of soil between each 3-inch layer of clippings.

Q. Can I spread dried manure on my lawn in the spring?

A. If you don't mind being asked to leave the neighborhood by summer. Boy, oh boy, that stinks—and it doesn't help.

Q. Will fresh horse manure tilled into the soil give you a better start with a lawn?

A. Year-old fresh manure isn't bad for a start, and in

52

many cases for a finish as well. Horses must be missing some part in their fertilizer factory because the weed seed goes right through. Why don't you just use a cheap lawn food?

Q. Who invented the lawn mower?

A. A sadist! It's funny that you should ask that question, because I asked my Grandma Putt the same thing thirty-eight years ago, and she knew the answer. She said, "Junior" (that's me), "Mr. Hills invented the lawn mower in 1868." So, now you know as much as I do.

Q. Can I color my lawn like the undertaker at the corner does in the winter?

A. I can't help but wonder if he is covering up anything besides brown grass. Sure, you can. There are several dyes that you can purchase from your garden center, which can be applied with a compression sprayer.

Q. What good does soap do for your lawn?

A. Makes it clean to begin with; next, it discourages insects, encourages growth because it breaks up compaction, and last and most important, it helps control lawn diseases before they get a start.

53

Q. How often and how deep do you plug your lawn?

A. About once a year in the fall and 2 to 3 inches deep should do the trick. By the way, rent a plugger. Don't bother to buy one.

house plants

Seventy-five to eighty million homes or apartments have a friendly house plant or two living or trying to live. It seems to me from my mail and conversations that the fault here is with most of you, not with the plant. You must always remember, *you* invited the plants to your house or office, they didn't tap you on the shoulder as you walked by and beg to go along. So it's your responsibility to make them feel welcome and safe. They in turn will do everything in their power to please you.

Next, let's clear up an old adage that simply is not true. And that is that some people just can't grow plants. That's foolish. If you take the time to spend with your green friends, and the patience to wait for them to do their thing, and last but not least, the

55

persistence to stick with a sick plant till death do you part, anything will grow. There are a few fundamentals for you to remember and then everything will grow right for you.

Heat

Just remember 62 degrees low, 74 degrees high.

Humidity

That's moisture, in case you forgot. 40 percent to 60 percent is best, and both you and your plants will feel well. Indoors, lack of it kills more plants than overwatering or overfeeding. From September to December, mist the foliage once a day with a weak solution of tea; twice a day from January to April. You can also set glasses of water, trays of wet sand or gravel, aquarium or other methods of moisture near your plants.

Light

When indoors, your plants need the same length of daylight or light year round as they get on the longest day of the year. The amount varies and is based on where your plants grow in their normal habitat.

56

Water

Heaven sent is best, well water is second best. Third best is water collected by refrigerators and dehumidifiers or that given off by your airconditioner.

When you water is when the plant wants a drink. And you can learn this by remembering the song lyrics, "Getting to know you, getting to know all about you." Before you invite a plant to come and live with you, make darn sure you can keep it happy.

Food

Plants get as hungry as you do, and the bigger they grow the more they eat. So feed them constantly. Feed boy plants with boy food (high-nitrogen foliage food) and girl plants with girl food (any flowering plant food), a little bit every time you water.

Just remembering these few things will help make your plants happy.

Q. How can I turn my black thumb green?

A. Paint it. Everyone has a green thumb; you were born with it. It's just that some thumbs ripen sooner than others. Pride, patience, and persistence, along with practice, are the only necessary ingredients to turn any thumb green.

Q. Which plants are really house plants?

57

A. Any plant that grows in the house is a house plant. If a maple tree was happy growing in your living room, it would be a house plant. If you can re-create the normal living conditions of any plant in your home, it can survive.

Q. *Can I grow fruits and vegetables indoors?*

A. Sure you can. What do you think those little orange, lemon, and lime trees, not to mention avocado trees, tiny tomatoes, cucumbers, and so on, are doing? All you have to remember is that the plant's comfort is what counts.

Q. *Does talking to plants really work?*

A. Don't ask me. Ask one of your plants. You already know where I stand—close! My fern is hard of hearing.

Q. *Is it true that plants that are for sale in supermarkets are not as good as those available in plant shops?*

A. Heck, no. They both buy from the same sources, and that's a fact! It's what happens after they arrive. The produce man doesn't have the time a plant man does, so the plants have to wait in line with the cabbages and the cucumbers.

58

Q. Are there places inside where plants won't grow?

A. Airtight closets, inside the oven, a closed refrigerator, and a hot furnace. Outside of those few places, no.

Q. How do I go about picking plants for my apartment or house?

A. How high is high? How long is long? Same kind of question. First, you must have a budget. You must know the night temp and day temp; you have to have a near-perfect idea of the percentage of humidity, light exposure of each room and each part of each room. Be sure you know if you have air conditioning, humidifier or dehumidifier; do you have gas, coal, wood or oil heat? Would you consider your furniture modern, colonial, contemporary, oriental, or Spanish? Do you travel a lot, have large parties? How's your physical and mental health? With these questions in mind, buy what fits.

Q. How come all plants that I purchase have bugs?

A. Because you have been visiting dirty plant shops. If a shop does not look clean, smell clean, or feel clean, don't go in—or if you do, don't bring anything out.

Q. I am on welfare, don't have much money, but

would like some plants. Which ones don't cost much, grow fast, and won't die?

A. The ones you are looking for are watermelon, squash, cantaloupe, cucumber, zucchini squash, any one of which makes a great house plant. Chickweed and wandering Jew also make inexpensive plants.

Q. Is it true that old people and foreigners can grow plants better than young Americans?

A. Ten years ago I would have said yes, but not anymore. The younger generation is fast learning that ecological management and knowledge are necessary for survival. Foreigners and older Americans had a taste of necessity during the depression.

Q. Where do most house plants come from?

A. From heaven, the stork brings them. Most of our tropical house plants come from Honduras to Florida and California, and then on to us.

Q. What's the difference between cactus and succulents?

A. To touch is to know; that's all, just thorns. They eat, sleep, and think the same.

60

Q. Is it true you should not buy plants when the temperature is below freezing?

A. Plants should never be exposed to temperatures below 50 degrees. If you can guarantee this, then you can buy and transport them at any time.

Q. Are plants grown in plastic pots better than those grown in clay pots?

A. If you are the commercial grower and paying the freight to ship, they are. But I prefer that you put your plants in clay work shoes and then set them down into the beautiful decorative planters, so you can change their wardrobe from time to time.

Q. What do you think of buying through mail order?

A. There are good and bad in any business. I have run into both, but never the same one twice.

Q. This may seem like a stupid question, but what is the best kind of top to put on a plant counter I am building?

A. Not to me, it's not. Cover the counter with metal, glass, plastic, or Formica so that it can be kept super-clean and free of germs and insects.

Q. What tools do you really need if you are going to have a great many indoor plants?

61

A. I have three bent forks for rakes, five spoons with the sides bent over in varying sizes to use as shovels and scoops, two sharp knives, a pair of tweezers, a toenail clipper for cutting stems, scissors, and a razor blade in a cork. That should do you.

Q. *Can you have too many plants in a room?*

A. Only if you can't take care of them or they affect lighting conditions that would hurt other plants or if you can't move about comfortably.

Q. *Is it true that you should never have plants in an infant's room?*

A. That's only true if the plants are dirty or buggy, but then that's true with plants in a grown-up's bedroom, too.

Q. *Have you ever seen a soil sample under a microscope? What are all those bugs?*

A. More than I care to count. As for the bugs, your guess is as good as mine. Some of them are good microscopic bacteria that give the soil its grow power, while others are bad ones.

Q. *Where can I find a book or a chart that tells me which plants go with what decor?*

A. Take a look at all the home-decorating magazines. You will see what you are looking for aesthetically, but in most cases it is deadly for the plant. Use your own imagination.

Q. Should you test house-plant soil for anything other than acidity?

A. No, it's not necessary.

Q. What is the best soil-test kit?

A. A cheap one. Sudbury has a large price range, and a kit can be purchased at most garden centers.

Q. Is garden soil good to pot plants?

A. I use it and don't have too much trouble. Just keep your eyes open for insect problems, and treat immediately.

Q. What's a good house-plant mix?

A. Equal parts of garden soil, peat moss, or sawdust and sand or perlite. Most commercial planter mixes will do just fine.

Q. What kind of soil does cactus like?

A. I have pretty good luck with a heavier soil mix and sand.

Q. *Are ashes good to mix up with soil for plants?*

A. Sure they are, but don't get carried away. A little goes a long way. Two handfuls to the bucket of soil mix.

X

Q. *Can sawdust be used in place of peat moss?*

A. I know lots of growers who do use it. However, you will have to feed a little more often until the sawdust begins to decay.

Q. *What good will coffee grounds do for plants? And should you mix them into soil for repotting?*

A. Coffee grounds help keep the soil loose, and build up acidity for plants that like rich soil, such as citrus, azaleas, and gardenias.

Q. *Are eggshells good to put into the soil?*

A. Again, they are only a soil conditioner. They only help in heavy soil.

Q. *Can I use sandbox sand for rooting cuttings?*

A. If you mean beach sand, no. The plants prefer sharp sand (builder's sand). Beach sand packs together.

Q. *Explain the difference between peat moss,*

64

sphagnum moss, perlite, and vermiculite, and what they are used for.

A. Peat moss is a fine, muck-base decomposed plant material. Sphagnum moss is a coarser, fibrous moss that almost looks like dried seaweed. Perlite is an expanded rock material, while vermiculite is a layered insulation material. They are all excellent soil conditioners and rooting medias.

Q. How do you steam-sterilize soil?

A. Any way you can. Boiling water poured over it will generally do the trick, or steam for 2 hours under a canvas cover.

Q. Does baking soil make it clean?

A. Sure it does. 250 degrees for one hour, or until a potato is tender.

Q. Do you have to have several different kinds of plant food?

A. Most of you do. A recent survey shows that you have between six and eight different brands of plant food sitting on your shelf. That's a waste. I suggest you have only two—one for boy plants and one for girl plants. I will explain before you think I am nuts. The way to tell the difference is not by lifting the plant's leaves. If a plant flowers, fruits, or vegetables, I consider it a girl and feed it with a flowering plant food called Bloomin. If, on the other hand, the plant is all foliage, it's a boy in the garden world, and boy plants are fed with a foliage food called Substral Earth Food.

Q. Can you make your own plant food?

A. Sure you can, but it isn't quite a full diet for your plants; and also don't overdo. This is the one my Aunt Florence uses.

> To one (1) gallon of warm water add
>
> ½ teaspoon ammonia
> 1 teaspoon Epsom salts
> 1 teaspoon saltpeter
> 1 teaspoon baking powder

Q. How often should you feed plants?

A. I feed every time I water. That's what you read, every time you water. The plant food I use says to add a capful per quart of water every time you do. I also add 3 drops of liquid dish soap per quart every time. If your plant food does not have these instructions, then I suggest you add 10 percent of the recommended rate and use every time.

Q. I heard that birth-control pills are good for plants. Is this true?

66

A. Estrogen pills only. And then they work great on all but the African violet and other leaves with hair (they bleach the color out of the leaves). To use on the rest of your plants, add one pill to 3 gallons of water and use once a month. Do not use on edible plants or you may notice a distinct change in your husband's appearance.

Q. *What do you use Epsom salts on?*

A. Epsom salts are magnesium sulphate and are used to deepen color of flowers or colored foliage, thicken petals and foliage, and stimulate more root growth. I add ¼ teaspoon per each 4-inch pot in the fall. For outside use, ½ cup per rose in the spring.

Q. *What do you think of fish emulsion plant food?*

A. I think it "stinks" (smell only), but it sure does the job on orchids and the rest of the Hawaiian group —birds of paradise, antherium, and the like. Use fish emulsion sparingly as a little goes a long way.

Q. *What good is plant food made from seaweed?*

A. Seaweed plant food joins the ranks of the other natural plant foods available for your plants. It does as good a job as any of the others.

Q. *How can you tell if you have overfed your plants?*

67

A. Generally the leaves will wilt, shrivel, and be soft. If this occurs, keep pouring water through the soil to back it out, and pray.

Q. *Can I use lime on my house plants?*

A. If you are using liquid, it's ½ teaspoon per quart; dry, it's one cup per ½ bushel of soil mix and then test.

Q. *Is gypsum a source of calcium?*

A. You bet your grass and the rest of your plants it's calcium! I add one pound per bushel of soil mix and 3 tablespoons per 4-inch pot in spring and fall to my indoor house plants.

Q. *What do you feed cactus?*

A. Rattlesnakes, scorpions, tarantulas—I'm just kidding. Boy cactus gets boy food and girl cactus gets girl food. You tell the difference the same way as with other plants.

Q. *What do you feed orchids?*

A. I use Substral Bloomin, and then once a month I give them a treat and serve fish.

Q. *How often do you feed poinsettia?*

HOUSE PLANTS

A. They are fed like any other girl plant.

Q. *What is meant by acid plant food?*

A. That is a plant food that contains more salts than others. Azaleas, citrus plants, gardenias, and rhododendrons are the acid group. I use weak coffee once a month for my indoor plants.

Q. *What type of plant food do you use if you are growing plants by hydrophonics?*

A. I continue to use my same plant food and in the same manner—10 percent of the recommended rate.

Q. *How many hours of light do plants need indoors?*

A. The dark is the biggest fear of plants. I guess they are afraid the plant bogeyman will get them. Not all plants need the same amount of light for the same length of time. Plants vary in likes and dislikes as much as people do. Look in your local newspaper to find out what time the sun comes up on the longest day of the year (the first day of summer). Then study the light requirements of plants you wish to befriend and see if you have locations to make them happy. So you thoroughly understand, plants need the same amount and length of light indoors as they do outdoors.

69

Q. Which kind of lights should I buy for indoors?

A. Along with proper natural light, I use Duro-lites, 75- and 150-watt plant lights, as well as GE and Sylvania.

Q. What the hell difference does it make to the plants if they get red or blue rays?

A. The same difference it does to your body. Man, plant, and animal need sunshine to survive, and pure sunlight contains a perfect combination of violet, blue, orange, yellow, green, and red. Red light makes the plant grow up faster (mature), while the blues tend to make the plant short, fat, and have dark green foliage without too many flowers. So we must get a good mix of both. There are at least a dozen books that go into growing plants under lights. About the best I know is one by a friend of mine, Elvin McDonald, *The Complete Book of Gardening Under Lights,* and it's in paperback.

Q. How close should plants be to a light fixture?

A. A rule of thumb is 12 to 18 inches with 40- to 60-watt bulbs, but then I must remind you that I could probably write a whole book on this subject. The Duro-Lite Lamp Company at 17-10 Willow Street, Fairlawn, New Jersey, 07410 has a super little book for $1.

70

Q. Which window exposure is best for which plants?

A. I am only going to name a few of the more common plants for each location, so don't be offended if your favorite is not on the list.

Bright Light: South or West with a Sheer Curtain

African violet
Amaryllis
Aphelandra
Azalea
Baby's-tears
Cactus and
   succulents
Christmas cactus
Chrysanthemum
Citrus plants (all)
Croton
Cyclamen

Gardenia
Gloxinia
Hedera (ivy)
Hibiscus
Hoya (wax plant)
Jade plant
Jerusalem cherry
Kalanchoe
Lanpranthus
Pittosporum
Poinsettia
Yucca

Medium Light: East Window

Anthurium
Asparagus fern
Begonia
Bromeliad
Caladium
Chlorophytum
   (spider plant)

Dieffenbachia
   (dumb cane)
Dracaena godseffi-
   ana, sanderiana
Fiddle leaf fig
Fuchsia
Grape ivy

71

Hydrangea
Maranta
  (prayer plant)
Nephthytis
Orchids (all)
Palms

Peperomia
Piggy back plant
Pothas (marble queen)
Rubber plant
Schefflera
Wandering Jew

Shady: North Window

Aspidistra
Bamboo palm
Dracaena marginata
  and massangeana
Kentia palm

Nephrolepis
Philodendron
Sansevieria
Spathiphyllum

Q. *How can you tell when a plant doesn't have enough light?*

A. In most cases, lack of light is indicated by pale, yellowish foliage, few flowers, funny-shaped leaves. Leaves will begin to fall off from all over, growth almost stops, buds only half open. That enough symptoms?

Q. *Can plants get too much light?*

A. I don't know why folks seem to think all plants are night owls and want light 24 hours a day, but I will let you in on a little secret. Plants only grow when they get proper sleep in the dark. If they have stayed up too long, they will wilt just like you will, and their leaves will get burned spots on them.

Q. What does diffused light mean?

A. I have always been taught that it is spread out or toned down: you know, like putting a sheer curtain in front of a west or south window.

Q. Which is the best exposure outdoors in the summer for my house plants?

A. The same exposure we talked about for inside. Just remember, when we bring them inside we re-create the plant's normal living conditions.

Q. Will a humidifier that I installed myself keep enough moisture in the house for most house plants?

A. It will help, but it's still not enough for your plants. Lack of humidity shows up when the edges of the leaves turn yellow or brown, buds shrivel up, and leaves fall off all over. As a rule, a temperature of 70 degrees should be accompanied by 40 percent humidity. I suggest you get two or three inexpensive humidity gauges at your hardware store.

Q. What damage does a dehumidifier do to plants?

A. Your dehumidifier draws humidity out of the air. By the way, the water from your dehumidifier is super

73

for watering plants. Almost the best. Same with your airconditioner water.

Q. *Is it true that an airconditioner is bad for plants, not because of the temperature but something else?*

A. That something else is the same answer as above. It's kind of ironic. In the summer we like our homes at 70 degrees, and so do plants, but the way an airconditioner works, it draws the humidity out of the house, which kills plants. But if you were to put 40 percent moisture into the room for the plants' sake, the airconditioner would die.

Q. *Can I use my baby's vaporizer for moisture in the air for plants?*

A. That's a great idea; we do it all the time, even in small greenhouses.

Q. *How close to my aquarium should my plants be to do any good?*

A. On top, next to, and all around. The closer the better. By the way, you can water your plants with that water.

Q. *Does spraying the foliage really help?*

A. Yep, sure does—once a day from September to December and twice a day from January to May. I

74

use a weak solution of tea in my Hudson Cordless electric sprayer.

Q. *Is a room humidifier as good as a central one?*

A. It is for that room, but not for the rest of the house, you, or your plants, if any of you leave that room.

Q. *Does an air purifier help or hurt plants?*

A. Heck, any time you hold dust down or eliminate it, it helps you, your plants, and your pets. You bet it helps.

Q. *Will a pan of water on a register help my plants?*

A. I kicked over many a pan of water that was sitting on the floor register at Grandma Putts' on my way to the toilet in the dark. And my Grandma was the plant expert of experts.

Q. *If the foliage dries up, how do you get moisture back into it?*

A. First, water it with warm water, shower with soapy warm water; then, put a brick in the bottom of a waste basket, set the plant on the brick, pour boiling water into the waste basket. To make steam (don't touch the pot), cover the top with a towel and leave for a 3- to 4-minute steam bath.

75

Q. *When is the best time to mist plants?*

A. I try to mist just before we all go to sleep (plants, kids, and me and Ilene) and again before noon. Remember the tea. The tannic acid in tea helps the plants' digestive system; it's also a wetting agent.

Q. *If I give my plants a shower every day with soap (baby shampoo), will it help the foliage?*

A. Yeah! But don't get carried away. Every couple of days is enough, if you have to. I wash every two weeks unless a heavy smoker has spent some time at the house.

Q. *Is gas heat bad for plants?*

A. Not unless you've got a leak, and then it is a real killer (plants, pets, and people).

Q. *Is it true that if you burn a fire in your fireplace, plants will die?*

A. Hell, no! Whoever told you that? If you were to have the plant on the hearth where it could cook, then it might die; but heat is heat.

Q. *What temperature do plants like best?*

A. As a rule most house plants like between 62 degrees at night and 74 degrees during the day, and so should you.

76

Q. What do people mean when they speak of proper air circulation for plants?

A. The same thing they mean when they tell you that you should have good air circulation. It means to move the air around in a room. That's why you have cold-air returns in your home. I often let a small oscillating fan run in the winter to move more air.

Q. What makes my plants grow crooked all the time?

A. You don't take them for a walk every day. Turn the pots at least half a turn each day, so that they get the same light exposure all over.

Q. How can you tell when it's too hot for plants?

A. When it's too hot for you. If you feel uncomfortable, so will your plants. First, the leaves will wilt, dry up, fall off from the top; then the roots will rot. 70 to 74 degrees is plenty high enough for both of you.

Q. What are the symptoms of plants that are too cold?

A. The leaves will immediately droop, become grayish (almost black overnight). They'll also look like they have goose bumps.

Q. Is water from a water softener bad for plants?

A. You can bet your pots on it, 'cause that's all you

77

are going to have left. The plants will be dead. Take the water out ahead of the softener.

Q. How do you purify water for plants?

A. Poke small holes in the bottom of a washed-out quart milk carton and fill half full of agricultural charcoal. Add shells from a dozen eggs and run water through this. Most of the salts will be gone (white powder on soil and pots).

Q. Is water from my defroster, dehumidifier, snow, and rain all the same?

A. Can't find much better, unless you have a pipeline to heaven. I never thought of that before. I wonder if holy water works better?

Q. How often do you water plants?

A. When they need it. Depends on the season, your house, the plant, and your memory. As a rule, I water when the soil feels dry to my touch at least an inch or two down into the soil.

Q. When do you water indoor plants?

A. I try to water in the morning, because that's when I am thirsty.

78

HOUSE PLANTS

Q. Which is the best way to water—top or bottom?

A. When it rains from hell, I will water from the bottom.

Q. How often do you water a terrarium?

A. When the soil looks dry, remove the cover and feel it. If you can't get your hand in, find some way to get a soil sample up.

Q. What's the best way to water a terrarium?

A. With a plastic straw. Mix water, food, and soap just as though you were going to water regular plants. Then place a straw in the water and cover the end with your thumb. Remove the straw from the water, place down into the terrarium, and remove your thumb. Not bad, eh?

Q. Why do you always say to add soap to water?

A. Soap makes water wetter, bugs don't like the taste of it, and I believe in clean soil. Dirt is filthy, and my plants and I don't use dirt.

Q. Are those water meters, gauges, and sticks any good?

A. Darn right, they are! If you have the cents, they make lots of sense.

79

Q. What's a nice, simple way to water plants when you are on vacation?

A. With someone else's hands, or you can buy some great watering devices.

Q. How often should you water hanging baskets?

A. Use the same rule as for plants with no hangups.

Q. How do you control ants?

A. Chlordane, Diazinon.

Q. How do you control aphids?

A. Malathion.

Q. How do you control mealy bugs?

A. Kelthane, Malathion.

Q. How do you control cut worms?

A. Chlordane, Diazinon.

Q. How do you control nematodes?

A. Chlordane, Diazinon, sugar.

Q. How do you control leaf rollers?

A. Kelthane, Malathion.

80

Q. *How do you control red spiders?*

A. Kelthane, Malathion.

Q. *How do you control sow bugs?*

A. Chlordane, Diazinon.

Q. *How do you control spring tales?*

A. Chlordane, Diazinon.

Q. *How do you control thrips?*

A. Kelthane.

Q. *How do you control millipedes?*

A. Chlordane, Diazinon.

Q. *How do you control centipedes?*

A. Chlordane, Diazinon.

Q. *How do you control white flies?*

A. Kelthane.

Q. *How do you control snails and slugs?*

A. Zectran, but do not use near foodstuffs.

81

Q. *How do you control leaf miners?*

A. Kelthane, Malathion.

Q. *How do you control gnats?*

A. Kelthane, Malathion.

Q. *How do you control earwigs?*

A. Malathion.

Q. *How do you control cockroaches?*

A. Chlordane, Diazinon.

Q. *How do you control crickets?*

A. Chlordane, Diazinon.

Q. *How do you control caterpillars?*

A. Thuricide.

Q. *What can you do to stop crown rot?*

A. Terban.

Q. *What can you do to stop stem rot?*

A. Terban.

Q. What can you do to stop mildew?

A. Benomyl.

Q. What can you do to stop mold?

A. Zineb.

Q. What can you do to stop sodium salt damage?

A. Use gypsum.

Q. What can you do to stop leaf spot?

A. Phaltan.

Q. What can you do to stop anthacnose?

A. Maneb.

Q. What can you do to stop damping off?

A. Thiram.

Q. What can you do to stop botrytis?

A. Zineb.

Q. Which plants are best indoors for hanging baskets?

83

A. Lest you forget—any plant that grows outside can grow indoors. Plants best suited for hanging baskets are fantana, Christmas cactus, wandering Jew, fuchsia, spider plant, strawberry begonia, hoya, ivies, and any of the melon or squash plants, and a cucumber thrown in.

Q. *Which plants would you recommend for terrariums?*

A. This may seem as if I am pulling your leg, but I am serious. Any weed that grows under trees or shrubs like chickweed, or moss, wild ferns, small toadstools, lichens, coleus, wandering Jew, begonias, African violets, and peperomias.

Q. *What plants would you pick for a dark room?*

A. *Aspidistra,* Bamboo palm, *Dracaena marginata, Dracaena massangeana,* Kentia palm, Nephrolepis, *Philodendron, Sansevieria,* and *Spathiphyllum.*

Q. *I am a traveling bachelor. Which plants would you recommend for me?*

A. How about a tomato? Well, I tried. Well, Don Juan, any plant that likes it cool, dim, and damp, which ends up with rex begonias, wax begonias, and ferns. A stag horn should fit your way of life or maybe a bird's-nest fern. Get the picture?

84

Q. Which plants can I start indoors from seed?

A. Any plant that has seeds you can start from seed indoors.

Q. How do you do root cuttings?

A. There are hard and soft wood cuttings. For complete instructions on when, how, and why, you must purchase a package of Rootone rooting hormone, and with it you get the best instructions. Honest, Injun!

Q. How long do bulbs have to cool before you can plant them?

A. Bulbs have got to cool at below 40 degrees for 10 to 12 weeks. You can cool in the refrigerator or underground.

Q. Which bulbs grow indoors?

A. All of them.

Q. Can you give me a list of things that can go wrong with house plants and how to spot them?

A. I will give you a few of the common problems and how to spot them.

Ends of leaves turn black: plant was in a cold place too long.

Ends of leaves turn brown: plant was in a warm, dry draft or not enough humidity.

Leaves just wilt: room is too hot, or the plant wants a drink, or you have a gas leak.

The mature leaves turn yellow and fall off: plant is starving to death.

The little tap leaves turn yellow: plant needs iron and more light.

Leaves fall off from the bottom: you are overwatering, and plant does not get enough light.

Leaves fall off from the top: not enough water and percentage of humidity is too low.

If the plant stops growing but looks pretty good: too much light and outgrowing its pot.

Q. *When do you transplant a house plant?*

A.   When its roots (feet) grow out through the hole in the bottom, or when they just seem to stand still.

Q. *Why do all the plants I transplant die?*

A. Because they went into shock. Water the plant 24 hours before transplanting, soak the new clay pot for one hour before, and use damp soil. Feed right after with a plant hormone food.

Q. *Do plants really like music?*

86.

A. They sure do; anything with a bass beat that you can feel physically.

Q. *Talking to plants is just a fake, right?*

A. Moses talked to a burning bush and Christ to a fig tree. You can talk to a flat tire or a cake that flops.

Q. *I saw you use a pest strip for insect control in house plants, on TV. How does it work?*

A. If you have lots of plants, just hang one close by. If you have a few spread out, cut the strip into 1-inch squares. Drill a hole into the end, and put a stick into the hole so that it looks like a lollipop. Place one in each pot.

Q. *What good does giving plants people names do?*

A. It makes me remember each one easier; I flunked Latin twice. Besides, you can't call them all "Hey, you" when carrying on a conversation.

Q. *Why do the blossoms on my gardenia fall off?*

A. The gardenia (*gardenia jasminoid* or Veitchii) does not want the temperature to drop below 60 degrees, no surprise breezes, or sudden temperature drops. It likes a lot of humidity, which you don't have in the wintertime. It likes a real, rich composted mixture of leaves, peat moss, sand, and manure.

Gardenias are best planted in pots and set outside on the patio in the summer when the threat of frost is gone and—WOW—will they fill the air with perfume. The younger a plant, the more flowers. Two- to three-year-olds do the best.

Q. Why don't my African violets bloom after the original flowers fall off?

A. African violets (*Saintpaulia*) are a snap to grow if you remember two things. First, they are a girl plant, a real bloomer, which needs lots of attention but not a great deal of care—there is a difference. To begin, keep the soil damp, not wet and don't let it dry out. Water from the top, just as you would any other blooming plant. Use 10 percent of the recommended rate of any African violet plant food in your watering water, with 3 drops of liquid dish soap per quart. Rain water, snow, defroster water, air conditioner runoff, or dehumidifier water are the best. You should feed the plant every time you water. Mist foliage with warm water to help humidity, which it likes at 40 to 50 percent. Heat should be 65 degrees to 74 degrees indoors, with 12 hours of good bright light, which should be 12 inches from plants. Grow your plants in clay pots and show them off in plastic, metal or glass. Violets love to be root bound. Any new growth (side shoots) should be cut off with a sharp knife and planted in its own shoes.

88

Q. Why do the stems of my large, lower leaves turn brown and break or rot off?

A. You would rot or break off if your arms rubbed on a rough old pot edge for long enough. I take an old wax candle and rub the dickens out of the edge to make it smooth. I also constantly remove older foliage to start new plants.

Q. When do you divide an African violet?

A. I remove any new crowns that appear as soon as they look as if they can take care of themselves in a 2¼-inch clay pot, which is clean and has been soaked for at least an hour or so. Make sure that the added soil is also damp and that the plant has been watered at least 24 hours before.

Q. How do you divide violets?

A. With an extremely sharp knife. Simply cut the newer crowns away from the older plant, keeping as much soil as is necessary and some roots to insure a good start. I keep my newly planted violets lightly shaded for a week.

Q. Should African violets be allowed to rest and for how long?

A. When they naturally stop blooming I let them rest,

89

give them a physical, transplant, and then let them start again.

Q. What do they mean by letting a plant rest?

A. Producing flowers takes a lot out of a plant, so to let it rest, you can pluck off buds, take it out from under the lights, run the temperature just a little cool, 65 degrees, scrub the pot, maybe give it a little shot of epsom salt water, ½ teaspoon per quart. 2, maybe 3 weeks of rest will be enough.

Q. Can I get amaryllis bulbs to bloom more than once a year?

A. If you want to go to a lot of trouble you can, but nine out of ten chances it won't work. When it is through flowering, cut the foliage back to the bulb, set in a warm, bright window that is 75 degrees during the day and 70 degrees at night, feed and water as a girl. When you have full grown new leaves, stop food, water, and shut off the lights. Foliage will dry up. Cut it off and leave it dark; moisten from time to time until you see growth start again, then move into light, feed and water it, and pray.

Q. Can you grow amaryllis from seed?

A. Yes, and be prepared for a 2 or 3 year wait for flowers.

90

Q. Is an avocado the same as a Calavo?

A. Yes, the California growers promote avocados; Florida saw a need for merchandising their product under a different name, Calavo.

Q. What's the best way to start and grow an avocado tree?

A. Since the fruit is good-tasting and good for you, even if you are on a diet, buy several, and, by the way, the Florida fruit is just as good as the California fruit. Next, remove the brown hide from the pit. Place one or two pits in a glass of room temperature, weak tea with a dash of epsom salts making sure that the liquid is just 1 inch from the butt (the point is the head). Support it with tooth picks. Place in a dark cupboard for 5 days. Now, move into sun and let it grow till root hits the bottom of the glass and top growth has two real leaves. Transplant into 4-inch clay pot (that has been soaked) with warm, damp African violet soil, leaving about ¼ of the pit above the soil line. Water, feed, and treat like any other plant. When growth is 10 inches to 12 inches high pick out the middle growth and watch the plant branch. Let it grow to 6 inches and pinch it and so on. The others you can try by planting directly into soil to begin. Keep damp (soil). Humidity is a must.

Q. Whey do the spikes of my aloe plant get soft and spongy?

91

A. *Aloe vera* is also known as the first aid plant, hangover plant, and beauty plant. When the leaves are soft it means the plant needs water. When the leaves are firm and hard it has enough water. Aloe likes lots of light (west), dry air, and does not like the temperature to go below 55 degrees. Feed with any foliage food added to your water.

Q. Why won't azaleas bloom again in the house?

A. The azalea is a flowering shrub that blooms when the temperature is cool. Most of our homes are not. To keep the flowers longer, maintain temperature at 50 to 65 degrees, keep the soil damp, not wet. Feed any blooming plant food in your watering water. Azaleas can be planted in your garden and then brought into the house in the fall.

Q. Will aglaonema do well in the shade?

A. Yes—all of them; there are several in the family—commutatum, fransher, pewter plant, and silver king. An excellent selection for low light rooms, but it does well in sunlight also. Don't let room temperature go below 60 degrees and keep the soil damp, feed with foliage food.

Q. Why can't I keep baby's-tears going in my house?

A. You probably don't spank it hard enough. I may make a lot of folks mad, but then "the truth does hurt."

92

Baby's-tears are a weed—granted, an expensive one, but none the less a "W-E-E-D." All you have to do to understand how to grow this popular weed is to have chickweed in your lawn. It grows under shrubs and trees where it is cool, damp, and slightly dark. May I suggest that you dig your chickweed up and tell people it's baby's-tears—they will never know the difference and you will save money.

Q. Now look! I am not a nut, but I've just got to know if some one is pulling my leg. Is there such a thing as the singer's begonia, the Hitler begonia, and the critics' choice begonia?

A. They are stretching the truth a little on Hitler. The singer's begonia is an orange angle wing begonia called Wayne Newton and, like the guy, himself, is super. The so-called Hitler begonia is an Iron Cross begonia, and the critics' choice is a Rex begonia, referring to the film critic Rex Reed. The begonia is one of the most versatile plants available. All begonias prefer plenty of light and do well inside or out, they must be kept damp but not sopping wet, fed with a girl food, because of their color or flower (no, they are not gay). I said versatile because they are great for slightly shady rooms; they need 50 percent humidity and a minimum night temperature of 65 degrees.

Q. How long do you have to wait for a bird of paradise to bloom?

93

A. About as long as you do for a little girl—twelve years; though some develop earlier than others, 7 years seems to be about average. Birds of paradise like warm, humid, bright living conditions. Keep slightly damp and add your plant food to the regular watering water, 15 percent of any flowering plant food.

Q. *How long after a bromeliad blooms can I expect a new shoot?*

A. I sure hope you have lots of patience, because a year to a year and a half is average. Bromeliads, of which pineapple is the most famous, like it warm—74 degrees, humidity, 50 percent and up, plenty of bright light and fed regularly with any girl food. The soil should be light and loose; wood shavings and peat are best.

Q. *If cactus is so easy to grow, why do I have so damn much trouble with mine?*

A. Probably because you haven't gotten the point yet. Cactus is best ignored, placed in a bright western window, near heat. Water well and then don't water again until the meat feels soft (I use a blunt stick to gently poke). Succulents are the same. Keep the humidity down with cactus and feed with boy food. The soil mix should be a sandy loam.

94

flower gardens

I can honestly say I have never met a person who does not enjoy the beauty of a flower garden. The colors, shapes, and fragrances stimulate our imagination. Many of the newer commercial buildings have been designed with a garden built into the center, for a relaxing area for employees, and we often have architects design a garden-patio area around our new homes.

Flowers provide more than just something to take up space. They provide continuity between the other plants in the garden, act as a border, or control traffic; and some flowers protect other plants from insects, enhance construction design, and provide us with fragrance and color both indoors and out.

Those who are the least bit critical about the use of

flowers are not really suggesting that we abolish their use, but feel that this space can be better utilized for food. There are many flowers which, along with giving us beauty and fragrance, are also food, or can be used to make food or drink. Roses are great for jelly, wine, and in salads. Mums are used in chicken soup; violets, pansies, and roses can be candied. So, this argument is not valid.

If properly planned and planted, you can have flowers from February through November out-of-doors, and, of course, blooms can abound indoors every month of the year.

Flower growing is probably one of the simplest things to do in gardening, as most flowers can pretty well take care of themselves if planted properly. Almost all annual flowers whether grown from seed, plant, bulb, or clump need good, rich medium- to well-drained soil (they do not like to stand in water), with full sunlight for most to medium shade for some. Most flowers need but one good feeding a year and very little or no weeding or cultivating; they give minimum worry from insects and disease if you wash them occasionally with soap and water and a touch of Malathion. Whenever or wherever possible I use grass clippings to mulch even my flowers. Two inches of mulch is usually sufficient. The trick to keeping flowers aplenty in your garden is to pick bouquets and to pluck or pull off old blossoms.

There are three basic plantings: annuals (from seed or plant), which last a single season; perennials (from seed or clumps), which grow year after year;

and bulb types, which consist of tubers, tuberous root, corms, and rhizomes. All three types can and should be interplanted to provide a full and balanced supply of beauty.

Q. *We have just moved into a brand new home in a new subdivision which I am sure is a branch of Interstate 75 since all the clay (blue, black, brown, and gray) was used to build up our grade. But then even that wasn't enough, so they hauled in sand, muck, and heck knows what else. My problem is I have large pockets of each. How can I have a good flower garden?*

A. What are you complaining about? You ought to send one of your first bouquets to your developer with a note of thanks for providing you with the richest growing media. Clay is the richest soil in the world if you can break it up.

   Begin by taking some of the sand and muck along with grass and leaves and garden gypsum. Till and spade it into the clay area. Take clay, muck, leaves, and grass and till into the sandy area. Add sand, leaves, and grass to the muck and quit your complaining.

Q. *Jerry, we have built a good porous base in our clay property, but the water backs up from beneath. What's the solution?*

A. French. If you will buy, rent, or borrow a tree auger

97

that can be used on an electric drill or hand brace and drill holes 2 to 3 feet deep in many areas of your garden, and fill the holes with gravel, this should carry off excess water. These holes are called "French wells."

Q. *What makes green moss grow in my flower beds?*

A. Poor drainage. I am sure not many of your flowers do too well. French wells, in addition to adding good compost base (grass and leaves), will help here.

Q. *Do all flowers like the same soil or is it true that perennials and bulbs like clay better than rich soil?*

A. Clay is rich soil. All plants, as I have said before, want loose, porous, well-drained soil.

Q. *Is it a good idea to use plastic as a mulch in flower beds?*

A. I use plastic only in my perennial beds, as I seldom move them, but I don't use it in my annual and bulb area. Here I use grass clippings. By the way, I use roofing paper (tar paper) rather than plastic, as it seems to last longer and work better.

Q. *Can I buy one kind of fertilizer for all flowers?*

A. Yeah! I use any garden food, low in nitrogen, high in potash and phosphorus. For bulbs and perennials

98

I add stinky bone meal to the soil. During the growing season you can add your liquefied table scraps to the flower beds.

Q. Hot often do you feed flowers?

A. I feed everything in the spring, and then during the season I hand-sprinkle a high meal once a month.

Q. What are Epsom salts used for in the garden?

A. Epsom salts (magnesium sulphates) are used to deepen the color, thicken the petals, and increase roots. Use ¼ cup per 4 square feet of flower or vegetable garden in May.

Q. Can I really use household ammonia as a fertilizer, without hurting my plants?

A. Curiosity killed the cat and satisfaction might bring it back if it isn't hit by a truck on its way to look. You be darn careful. It's ½ teaspoon per gallon.

Q. How long will flowers last when you dry them?

A. If you spray them with five or six coats of hair spray, you should get a couple of years or more out of them.

Q. What's the best way to dry flowers?

A. I use 3 cups of borax and 1 cup of corn meal mixed. Place freshly picked flowers in a container that can be sealed. Cover with mixture, seal, and let stand for 4 to 5 days.

Q. *What are some good projects for children using plants and flowers?*

A. I like using fruit such as oranges, grapefruit, limes and lemons in projects with kids. Cut the fruit in half, clean out the meat, punch 2 or 3 holes in the skin. Fill the half shell with soil, place the seed taken from the fruit into the soil-filled shell and treat like any other house plant. The peel will harden up and become the pot.

Q. *Is a homemade greenhouse as good as a prefabricated one?*

A. I have seen some awfully good homemade ones, but, then, I have also seen some awfully bad ones. If they get the job done then they are all OK. I sure do like those prefabs, though.

Q. *Can I really use beer on my plants? Which ones?*

A. All of mine do fine on beer. I mix 5 parts of water to one part of flat beer and use the mixture as a watering base, instead of tea.

Q. *What is saltpeter used for in a garden?*

100

A. As a rule it is the base used in stump removers. A ½ teaspoon per gallon of water can be used to stimulate root growth. It is purchased as potassium nitrate in most drugstores. I suggest you have a sense of humor when you go to buy it.

Q. *I was given a gallon of seaweed plant food. Is it really plant food?*

A. It sure is and a darn good one, though it is very mild and slow acting. A friend of mine in Boston, Massachusetts, uses real seaweed as a mulch compost and has terrific luck.

Q. *How good is horse—— in a flower garden?*

A. Not really good in mine, unless it is a couple of years old. Man, it's mean stuff if it's too young. Horse—— is full of weeds and humus foliage, and makes my plants too tall.

Q. *How much and how often do you use lime in a flower garden?*

A. Same as in a vegetable garden—one pound per 100 square feet once every three years.

Q. *Our town offers sludge free. Is it good and safe for my plants and my family?*

A. I have followed closely the sludge tests being

101

conducted by the Environmental Protection Agency and leading universities, and it is working out absolutely great and safe. Use it; you can't beat the price. Sludge breaks up clay and makes grass, trees, and evergreens grow to beat the band; vegetables will, too.

Q. Why do my annuals dry out so much faster than my bulbs and perennials?

A. Because annuals are rooted more shallowly than the others. Mulch or water them lightly more often.

Q. Why do my flowers look so dismal after I water them, and some even get a white powder on them?

A. I find that watering with a soaker about one o'clock each afternoon, avoiding top-watering, makes my flowers happy and clean-looking. The white stuff is mildew which comes from poor water care.

Q. You always hear about people who have a brown thumb with house plants, but have you ever heard of an outdoor brown thumb?

A. Knock it off! Neither you nor anyone else has a nongrowing thumb. Hell, even I don't have a green thumb. I ripened all over. To have a green thumb outdoors, just remember The Big 4: (1) pick a recommended variety (for your part of the country and

102

soil) of good, fresh seed; (2) make sure your soil drains well and is, or is made, rich and loose with leaves, grass, and compost; (3) feed regularly with a proper garden food; (4) make darn sure you understand when, where, and how to water. There! That ought to ripen your thumbs.

Q. What the dickens is the difference between garden food and any other plant food?

A. I guess you would say a play on words. Garden food is for girl plants (as I've explained earlier, that's anything that flowers, fruits, or vegetables), and they want more potash and phosphorus and less nitrogen. So the formulas of dry garden food would look like this: 4–12–4, 5–10–5, 6–10–4, and so on; and a liquid like the one I use from Science Products is 10–52–17. Plants that just bear foliage need lots of nitrogen so I use a lawn food for trees, grass, and evergreens.

Q. How many different kinds of annuals are there?

A. I am just taking a shot in the dark on two counts. First, there are literally hundreds of varieties and cross combinations of varieties, so you should have no problem satisfying your taste. Second, if you mean is there more than one kind of an annual, the answer is no. An annual is a plant that lives its full life cycle in one season. A biennial is a plant that lives a lifetime in two years (maybe three if it's tough).

103

Q. It always seemed like a waste of time to make a plan each year for my annuals until I saw the results of a new shopping center in our town! I am now convinced. Where do I start?

A. You were not in an elite club. Most folks are content to hit and miss with annuals, as well as all the rest of their flower plantings; and from the looks of things, most of them continue to strike out year after year.

Your "garden" is a total picture. Everything should blend in with every other thing, complement, enhance, not be a group of "sore thumbs" sticking out. Your *home* is the most important, and we want to make it appear to fit into its surroundings. Trees should be properly located, evergreens should be the proper shape to look as if they are welcome, and your selection of flowers should tie it all together. I paint a little (not good, just paint), and I consider flowers as shading and accenting.

I am not a selfish person, but I do take into consideration my view out from my house as much as the view of a passerby. So I plant to please both views. Look at lots of pretty pictures for ideas, and then make them fit your taste and personality.

Q. I love hanging baskets, but they keep drying up on me. How can I prevent this?

A. Usually a hanging basket is under an overhang or in a shady spot, or in a spot where there is a dry breeze blowing at it all the time. I water more often with about a teaspoonful of liquid dish soap per gallon of warm water. I feed with liquid garden food, 10 percent of the recommended rate, every other time I water. I use a fishing swivel between the hook and the hanger so the planter can turn all the way around. Once a week I set my baskets on the ground for several hours in a northeastern exposure. I also exchange locations.

Q. When do you start your seed inside for annual flowers?

A. If you have a Gro-Varium (a specially designed tray with a plastic dome and soil-heating cable unit, made by Wrapon Company, and available at any garden store), start them in March; if not, in February, transplanting three times to insure stronger plants. Feed new and old plants with Garden Life Soluble Plant Food (10–52–17) by Science Products.

Q. Does the tea-and-refrigerator soaking really speed up flower seed?

A. I am the guy who pushes it the most. Soak for at least 18 hours.

Q. Which flowers are considered bug chasers?

A. The most common are marigolds, asters, nasturtiums, and mums.

105

Q. Give me a list of flowering annuals that like shade.

A. Why not try coleus, impatiens, lobelia, myosatis, calendula, browallia, nicotiana, pansy, salvia, balsam, begonia.

Q. We live at Cape Cod. What will stand the salty sea breeze?

A. Alyssum, petunias, lupine, dusty miller.

Q. Which of the annuals can you grow inside as house plants?

A. Any that will grow outside, if you re-create in your home the normal, sweet, soft day of June 15 (and I don't mean a thunderstorm, smart guy!).

Q. Which are biennial plants?

A. The most popular are pansies, hollyhocks, forget-me-nots, and foxgloves. These are planted in the fall, covered with soil and topped with straw, and arrive in the spring.

Q. Aren't perennials really weeds? or wild flowers?

A. There is no such thing as a weed. It's just a plant we haven't found a use for yet. Yes, they were wild flowers, and in some parts of the country some of them still are.

106

Q. I have stayed away from perennials because I have been told they spread all over your garden, almost like a weed.

A. That's a shame. I mean that you haven't enjoyed the beauty of perennials. Perennials are the best flowering investment you can make. Yes, they multiply, increasing your investment, but they only go where you let them.

Q. When do you plant perennials?

A. In warm climate, anytime they are available. In cold country, I prefer May for the most part in good, rich composted loam (leaves, sand, grass, sawdust), well drained.

Q. Can you send me a list of the blooming order of perennials?

A. Dear you: Here is your list of perennials in the order they bloom: *Early:* primrose, sweet William, violets, pinks, candytuft, creeping phlox, and bleeding heart. *Early Summer:* iris, shasta daisy, carnation, columbine, astilbe, peony, poppy, and gaillardia. *Mid-Summer:* lavender, heliotrope, platycodon, baby's breath, delphinium, and daylily. *Fall Blooming:* chrysanthemum, aster, lythrum, and helianthus.

Q. When is the best time to divide or move perennials?

A. In the spring where it's cold and in the fall in warm areas. I have my own way of dividing. First, my spade is razor sharp. I keep my shovels that way with a *#10 Bastard File.* In the late fall I take my spade and cut right through the perennials I am going to transplant, pull the spade out, and lightly cover the plant with light straw for the winter. In the spring I dig up only the half I am going to move; no shock, no mess. Also, I don't give up a season of blooms.

Q. How do you keep the weeds out of a perennial bed?

A. I use a chemical garden weeder or tar-paper mulch with decorative stones on top.

Q. Which are the best bulbs to buy—Japanese or Dutch?

A. Bulbs came from the Orient first, and they are now back in the business. I have good luck with both. I tend to lean toward Holland bulbs, but I think that's only due to Hans Brinker.

Q. For the last three years, our tulips have never had any flowers and start to grow in the winter. What are we doing wrong?

A. It's not what you are doing; it's what you did. Odds are you have them planted too close to a heated wall or planted them too early. Plant bulbs after a good

frost in an open, well-drained fertile soil, well composted. I suggest you dig them up and start over.
Also, they can be planted too shallow.

*Q. When is the best time to plant spring flowering
bulbs?*

A. Never plant them before there has been a good,
killing frost in the North, and not before they have
been refrigerated for ten weeks in warm-weather
areas.

Q. Which are the first bulbs to bloom?

A. As a rule, snowdrop and winter aconite in February and March; crocus and glory of the snow in
March and April; tulips (Fosteriana, Peacock, Kauf-
manniana, Red Emperor tulips as well) bloom in April
and May. Grape hyacinth, daffodil, and single and
double early tulips show off in April and May, along
with hyacinth and medium- and short-clipped daffodils. Darwin and Triumph tulips begin their display,
accompanied by Breeder tulips and Scilla. From May
through June the rest of the tulips, like Parrot, Col-
tage, Darwin and lily-flowered tulips, and last but by
far not least, Dutch iris.

Q. Can you really plant bulbs too deep?

A. You really can, and by the same token you can
plant them too shallow. Daffodils and hyacinths are

109

planted at 6 inches, tulips at 5 inches, and small bulbs at 3 inches.

Q. The stems on my tulips are big enough but don't seem to have any support. Why?

A. I would say you are guilty of planting your bulbs upside down. I have been asked on behalf of bulbs everywhere to tell you folks to plant the head up, bottom down.

Q. What is bulb food , and is it necessary to use a special one?

A. Usually an ordinary garden food with a liberal supply of bone meal, and no, it's not necessary. But it is a must to feed your tulips, etc., when they are blooming.

Q. How often do you have to dig up tulips?

A. I do it every three years, unless my bulbs aren't flowering or have small flowers. Then I move them.

Q. Do you have any suggestions for a plant in a hanging basket? I would prefer a bulb so I can use it over and over.

A. My favorite is widows tears (*Achimenes*). It loves hot weather but must come in before frost, and it comes from a rhizome.

110

Q. Can amaryllis be grown outside?

A. There are two types: belladonna lily and hippeastrum. Belladonna is for outside and hippeastrum for indoors.

Q. What's the most durable of the bulb-type plants?

A. You just can't beat the begonia, any type. They like heat, shade, dry, and somewhat dry. They also make great house plants.

Q. What's the toughest of the bulb-type flowers?

A. I don't think you can beat cannas or elephant's ears.

Q. When is the best time to plant tiger lily?

A. In early May, when the soil is warming up. This is the same with any lily. Don't forget, you can replant your Easter lily and expect blooms in July and August.

Q. My lilies just rot every year. Can they be diseased?

A. I would say that your lily patch is in a wet spot; lilies can't stand water.

Q. When do you transplant lilies?

111

A. In the early fall is the best time. Dig the clump carefully. Replant and feed with a mild liquid garden food.

Q. *Do iris lilies, glads, and begonias have to be dug up in the fall?*

A. Only begonias and gladioluses; dahlias and cannas must be dug and stored.

Q. *What do you do to bulb roots so they don't rot or dry out when they are stored?*

A. When the stem is yellow, dig the root and remove soil. Then I wash in a weak soil solution and let dry for 4 to 5 weeks, put them in a paper bag with Thiram, a fungicide, and shake like donuts. Now place them in a box of dry peat moss at 50 degrees.

Q. *I just can't afford all the dusts and sprays necessary for flowers. Is there one I can use?*

A. It's not a good idea to have too many sprays lying around anyway. I use a multipurpose garden dust from Science Products that can be made into a spray as well and is for food and flowers. The medication used is Malathion and Methoxychlor and Captan. And for soil problems, I use Chlordane or Diazinon.

112

Q. When do you take cuttings from geraniums?

A. Any time during the season if you are planning to grow them as house plants. You must take the last ones before frost gets them. Cuttings are taken from young growth 4 to 5 inches long, and all the leaves are taken off so it looks like a piece of asparagus. Dip the cut end into Rootone 1½ inches and then place in a 3-inch clay pot with African violet soil. Feed and water until growing well. Then transplant to a 4-inch pot and bury the pot in the ground. Before frost, remove pot and bring inside.

Q. How do you save geraniums?

A. Pull them out by the roots and store upside down in your garage until March 15, at which time you can cut ⅔ off the top back and ⅓ off the roots. Pot and begin to feed and water. When the threat of frost is gone, plant in the ground.

Q. Can geraniums be planted from seed?

A. Yes, they can. They germinate slowly, so start them indoors. The seed is not in every seed rack. They're called "Carefree."

Q. Can you take cuttings from coleus?

A. Right on. Pull a leaf and root in sharp sand. In the

113

fall dig the whole plant and pot. The same goes for impatiens.

Q. Can you transplant caladium for indoors?

A. Yeah, you can—but, boy, they look awful.

trees—flowering, shade, and fruit

We certainly are unappreciative of something that our life depends upon. Oh, I know, on a hot day in July you appreciate it for cooling you, and in May when it flowers you ooh and aah about its beauty, and in August and September you really appreciate its fruits. But the rest of the year you ignore it, bitch about its leaves falling or the sap dripping on your car, the bugs it attracts, the sewers it clogs. Not once do you put your arm around its shoulder and say, "Thanks for keeping me alive." A TREE! That's what I am talking about. Without trees you couldn't breathe because they provide your only source of oxygen.

That's it, folks—trees, grass, flowers, and shrubs keep you alive; and the way we treat them sometimes, I wouldn't blame them if they went on strike and held their breath.

Trees can also increase the cost of property you want to buy and increase the value of a home you want to sell. A mature tree can insure an additional $1,000 over other houses in the same block without trees. Try that on for size.

As I travel about, I see trees with broken limbs hanging from them, with no apparent effort on anyone's part to relieve the pain; eventually the tree dies, and the air gets a little thinner. I could chew grass for a week when I get started on this subject, and it always does my heart good to get a letter or question on the care of any tree. Trees don't demand a great deal of attention, but they do want some.

Always plant a tree where it is going to have room to spread out and up and not hit its head on telephone wires or bump its shoulders on the corner of the house. Don't plant a tree where it's got to stand knee deep in water or plow through your sewer pipes. Plan with a pencil before you plant with a spade. Spades don't have erasers.

Dormant-spray all trees in fall and spring, and if it's too high for your sprayer, con the neighbors into a community project and hire someone to get the job done. Feed all trees at least once in the spring. Shade trees can be fed with lawn food, and flower and fruit trees with garden food.

Remove, sterilize, and seal any structural damage

116

toot-sweet. Brace weak or split limbs and take any unusual-looking foliage to your nursery man at once for diagnosis and then treat. Since your life depends on them (the trees), you owe it to them to keep them healthy.

Q. When is the very best time to plant a tree, any tree?

A. Today you can plant trees twelve months a year. Potted, balled, and burlap trees can even be planted when you have to break the frozen ground with a pick. But for the most part late fall or early winter is best for balled stock.

Q. Is it OK to buy mail-order fruit trees?

A. It sure is. All my dwarf fruit trees come from Stark Brothers Nursery, and I have never had bad luck yet. Mail-order houses have a much larger assortment of fruit trees. Up until the last six years most home gardeners didn't have time for fruit trees, but that picture has sure changed.

Q. What's the biggest you suggest a tree be when planted?

A. With the new diggers (power), I can't say. They can move 30- to 40-foot-high trees the way you and I move a whip.

117

Q. *My next-door neighbor just got a box of trees from a catalog order and the roots weren't in dirt. He planted them, but will they live?*

A. Shade, fruit, nut, and flowering trees are sent mostly bare-root. Your local nursery will either pot them or plant them in fields for growing. Others package them with wet sawdust on the roots and place them in plastic bags. If he soaked them well and planted them properly, they will do just fine.

Q. *Can you plant bare-root trees in fall with good results?*

A. Late October and early November are just fine. Brace the trees with wire, wrap the trunk, mulch the base with leaves, and you got yourself some winners.

Q. *Cheez, have you ever seen the tap root on a pecan tree? Do you have to dig the hole that deep?*

A. Yep, I use a posthole digger. The pecan tree has a tap root longer (about four feet) than any other tree you can buy. They're certainly worth it.

Q. *Why do they call some trees wild trees?*

A. That's a terrible thing to say about any tree. The willows, soft maples, poplars, and soft elms have been tagged with this handle. I guess that's because they grow so fast and get into a lot of trouble. But

118

then, boys will be boys. By the way, I like that whole bunch and recommend them for what they are— active growers. (I was one as a kid.)

Q. Is it necessary to wrap the trunk of all newly planted trees?

A. I do, and after a year or two I change the wrap and leave it on for a third year. Tree wrap keeps the moisture in and prevents bark split and sun scald.

Q. What will grow in clay?

A. Any tree you see growing in your community. The trick is to do what landscape contractors do in that kind of problem spot—mound-plant. Build small hills in different locations where you want trees and then contour them. Plant your trees in the mounds, above the clay, and you will never lose a tree.

Q. What is the best type of soil for trees?

A. Most trees do well in a sandy loam to a good clay loam, but as a rule do not do well in heavy clay.

Q. Do I have to prune a newly planted fruit tree back? If so, how much?

A. The grower and I suggest one-third be cut back and generally just above a break. This stimulates

119

new growth. And, by the way, this includes large balled and burlap trees as well.

Q. Can trees make any real difference in reducing noise?

A. Yes, sir-re-bobbie, they can. Trees and shrubs act as an acoustical sponge. If you place your trees properly, you can reduce noise by 25 to 35 percent.

Q. Should fruit and nut trees be kept in a special area, or can you mix them up?

A. You can mix and match any tree or group of trees. The whole idea is to make the trees and your landscape compatible—the size, height, shape, color, and its commodity (fruit, nut or berry). I try not to put fruit trees too close to patio or play areas, for the safety of both people and trees.

Q. Do you have to brace all newly planted trees?

A. I always do. Brace against the prevailing wind. Try to pad the bark area with sponge rubber, rags, or some other soft material to keep the bark from being torn or rubbed off. I like to leave the stake on for at least one full season.

Q. Rabbits and mice eat the bark on my new trees. How do you stop them?

A. Wrap the bark with tree wrap right down to the soil; then place medium stones around the base in a circle. If the problem is really bad, make a wire collar out of hardware cloth and place around the trunk.

Q. *When is the best time to feed fruit trees?*

A. In light soil you should feed in March and April, but not in the summer. In heavy soil, feed in November and December when the soil is frozen. The snow and rain will carry the food down through the cracks, and the food will be waiting when the tree wakes.

Q. *Is liquid plant food better than dry for flowering crab trees?*

A. One is as good as the other if it is applied in the right place at the right time in the right way. Use a root feeder in March and April and use a recommended food for flowering trees. Feed trees out at the drip line.

Q. *What's the best way to water a tree?*

A. With a soaker base laid in a circle out at the drip line.

Q. *What do nut trees eat?*

121

A. Girl food, low-nitrogen garden food. Feed them in the spring.

Q. *When is the best time to prune a birch tree?*

A. In late June, as a birch is a bleeder and must be sterilized immediately with a solution of 2 table-spoons of household ammonia per quart of water, sloshed onto the wound. Then seal with pruning paint. Maples and walnuts are also bleeders.

Q. *When do you recommend pruning unwanted branches on flowering trees?*

A. Almost any time you have the time. I find early winter to be the best for me.

Q. *Is it necessary to prune trees every year?*

A. A well-manicured tree will be healthier and pret-tier than one that is left to go its own way. However, there may be seasons when they need no help.

Q. *Can you use wood chips made from limbs that you have taken from the same tree as mulch under-neath?*

A. You can use them if the limbs were removed for any reason other than being sick.

Q. *What do you think of iron plugs for trees?*

122

A. What this gardener is talking about are small capsules in a frame that looks like a flathead bullet. You drill holes in the trunk and tap in a capsule which breaks down and gives iron to the tree. I prefer any of the powder or liquid irons fed through the roots.

Q. How can you remove sap from tools?

A. Wipe off with alcohol and rub down with oil each time after using. Rust on tools doesn't do your trees or tools any good.

Q. How do you repair bark split from the ground up to the first branch?

A. That's called "southwest bark split," which is caused in the winter months when the bark thaws out on the sunny side of the tree and swells up and splits. Remove loose bark, sterilize, and seal. If it's a small tree, wrap with tree tape; if it's a large tree, protect in winter with a strip of tar paper taped to the southwestern side of the tree.

Q. My kids ran into a maple tree with the lawn mower. How do you stop this?

A. Give your youngsters driving lessons on a mower. Take a sharp knife and cut the rough edges of the bark back to undamaged bark, making the edges smooth. Sterilize and seal.

123

Q. *We had a colony of carpenter ants in a tree. We got rid of the ants but are left with an empty ant house in the trunk. What do we do?*

A. Because you have to look at it, I will say fill the cavity with cement. First, clean the cavity of all loose wood and chips. Sterilize and seal the inside. Then mix some ready-mix and fill.

Q. *Can a tree that was struck by lightning be saved?*

A. The only thing you can do is remove broken limbs, bark, and ruined foliage. Sterilize, seal, and pray. Only about 50 percent make it.

Q. *Can I safely cable a tree myself?*

A. Oh, I think so. Make sure you use good-sized eyes and heavy enough cable. Use a turnbuckle, not a straight cable.

Q. *Why does my elm tree leak sap all the time?*

A. It's called "wetwood bleeding." The tree is sick inside and needs a tree doctor. Do not mess around. Call the *man.*

Q. *Should you cut off the big lumps on the side of a peach tree?*

A. No, just leave them alone. Odds are this kind of

lump is a scar from an old war wound that has cal-
loused over.

Q. Can I move an apple tree?

A. Just the way you would any other tree. It just won't
(and should not) have apples the first year (even if
you have to pick the blooms off).

Q. Why are dwarf fruit trees so weak?

A. That's not a nice thing to say. After all, they carry
the same load as their big sisters carry per branch. I
make a point of bracing the limbs as the fruit grows
bigger.

*Q. How much room should you have between dwarf
fruit trees?*

A. I like 10 feet either way. This is to give both the tree
and me room to work.

Q. Do you dormant-spray all fruit trees?

A. I should say so. All woody caned trees should be
dormant-sprayed in fall and winter, for sure.

Q. Do you have to have two fruit trees to get fruit?

A. It helps, but it's not really necessary. The birds,
bees, and wind and whatnot help.

125

Q. Will the shoots that grow out of the roots of flowering crabs and some other trees hurt the tree?

A. They don't do it any good, and they look like hell. I remove them over and over and over.

Q. Give me the names of good, fast-growing trees that I can plant at our cottage.

A. Here we go. Every time I read a trade book or paper, they say don't plant weed (fast-growing trees), but I am all for them. Any kind of tree I can get—and afford. If you find one you don't like, you can remove it or not plant it again. Chinese elm (brace the crotch), mulberry (dirty), corkscrew willow (I love it), weeping willow (its roots grow into the sewers), cottonwood, poplar, hedge apple (the fruit discourages roaches), hackberry (shallow rooted; good for mound planting on clay), and silver maple. That ought to keep you hopping.

Q. How do you keep borers out of peach trees, birches, and God knows what else?

A. He does know what else. I apply para-dichlorobenzene moth crystals on the soil.

Q. What's the best fruit-tree spray?

A. I use one that combines Methoxychlor, Malathion, and Captan. I don't have a problem.

126

Q. *What do you use to kill grubs under a tree?*

A. I use Chlordane or Diazinon.

Q. *Is there a good all-purpose spray for trees?*

A. The same thing you use on your fruit trees.

Q. *Can you keep fruit from forming on ornamental crabs?*

A. Spray with plant birth control Amid-Thin.

Q. *Is there a cure for Dutch elm disease?*

A. Not as far as I know, but they are working on it. Feed your elms, spray, and prune properly, and they should be OK. The elm bark beetle attacks weak, sick trees.

Q. *Are systemic insecticides effective and safe?*

A. They're darn good, and used properly and on the right trees as recommended, they are safe.

Q. *Which of the magnolias are hardy?*

A. Star and Purple Flower are pretty good. The flowers are early and a mess when they drop, but the foliage and color make up for this shortcoming.

127

Q. *Why can't I get a dogwood to bloom? As a matter of fact, I have a tough time just keeping it alive.*

A. The fragile dogwood must be protected from the southwest wind if it is to bloom. Wrap the trunk and screen the crown if it is exposed.

Q. *Why do they call the maytree a bird's paradise?*

A. Because it has a ton of berries to feed on. You would like to also. It looks good and smells good.

Q. *What's the name of the metalic bronze maple tree?*

A. It's called Schwedler's maple. It's a real regal tree for a front lawn.

Q. *What's the maple with the white edge?*

A. Variegated leaf maple, a real showpiece, grows to about 30 feet, not really fast, but worth the wait.

Q. *Are any of the elms safe from the Dutch elm disease?*

A. Yep! Hybrid elm (*Ulmus Americana*) will fill the bill.

Q. *Why do my mountain ash limbs all bend over and look like hell all the time?*

128

A. Don't feed so much with lawn food. Use a garden food, and remember that this tree doesn't like wet or heavy soil.

Q. *Which is the best locust tree for a shade tree?*

A. I have to cast my vote for the Moraine, hands down.

Q. *Is the beech fast or slow growing?*

A. Slow, like its brother the hickory, and both have hard heads.

Q. *What's the name of the tree that grows kitty corner from your home?*

A. That's a basswood tree or better yet, American linden. Ilene wants that in our yard, but I've got no room for a 60- to 80-footer. That's what it's going to get to. Next door, my neighbor has its little cousin, little-leaf linden, which is as pretty, almost, and goes only to 40 feet.

Q. *How do you get birch trees to get white bark?*

A. You wait for them to reach puberty, when they are about five or six years old.

Q. *How do you control birch-leaf minors?*

A. Spray early with Malathion and keep it up.

Q. *What's with the birch borer?*

A. He likes birches and son of a birch. Use moth crystals in the fall and spring.

Q. *Does the flowering peach have peaches?*

A. Not that you can write home about. Boy, is that a good-looking tree when it flowers.

Q. *Do you, or should you, wrap the trunks of crab trees?*

A. I have my Zumi and my weeping crab trunks wrapped with tree wrap, and they were dormant-sprayed.

Q. *How do you feed flowering trees?*

A. Bore 2-inch holes 12 inches apart, 8 inches deep, in a circle at the weep line, and pour a mixture of half sand and garden food into each hole in the spring. Shade trees are fed the same way, but I use lawn food. Make sure you run a spreader over the grass after you feed, or you will have bright green clumps in a circle.

Q. *What's the best way to get rid of a stump without digging?*

130

A. Drill a series of holes—the more the merrier. I would like them large and as deep as you can drill. Now, fill them with a commercial stump remover that contains saltpeter (potassium nitrate) and leave for one year, plugged. At the end of one year, remove the plugs, pour in kerosene, let set for an hour or so, and light. The stump will smolder away to ashes.

vegetables and small fruits

I just can't help but wonder why we took so long to learn what people in most other nations discovered centuries ago—that man must tend the earth if he expects to continue to live on it. Whenever any of my friends visit Great Britain, France, Germany, or other European nations for the first time, they are amazed by the fact that almost every single home has a garden and, in most cases, no lawn—just a garden—and they wonder why. Well, as we have now discovered, sort of the hard way, a garden is for survival, not looks, to most of this old world, and it has just come home to us in the past few years. Many of us now plant a garden out of necessity because we can't afford the inflated price for someone else to do the hard work. Most of us have discovered that it's not as hard as we imagined; in fact, it's fun, healthy, and rewarding—physically, psychologically, and financially.

Anyone can have a garden. Heck, I know folks who grow food in an alley 'cause that's the only place there is soil. Others grow food in ashcans on roofs, or in boxes. If you have a patch of soil, you are ahead of most folks. If you are going to have good, fresh food, try to place your garden patch in a well-lighted spot, where no water stands. Make sure you remember that each plant you grow needs room, just like you do, so don't crowd him or her. Feed your plants regularly and keep them clean and neat. Watch for trouble and act at once. Remember: *Never put off until tomorrow what should be done today in a garden.* Or there won't be a garden tomorrow.

Q. Where is the best place to grow vegetables?

A. Any place you can get an 8- to 10-inch depth of soil together—wooden boxes; wastepaper baskets; tubs; cement blocks; wooden frames on a roof, driveway, or walk.

Q. What kind of dirt do you need for a good garden?

A. To begin with, the word is soil, not dirt. Soil is a productive composition of decayed materials such

133

as leaves, grass clippings, sawdust, weeds, and fallen trees, while dirt is a collection of filth. Any well-drained soil will do nicely. This means a soil that water does not stand in pockets on top of, not pure sand that will not hold any moisture at all.

Q. I live in a new subdivision where heavy clay was used as backfill, and I just can't get a good garden started. What will really break up the clay?

A. You can add 50 pounds of garden gypsum per 1,000 square feet in the fall and spring. In the fall put a mixed layer of leaves, grass clippings, ashes, wood chips, sand (builders'), or peat moss 6 inches thick and sprinkle 15 pounds of garden food per 500 square feet. Let set all winter. In the spring spade or roto-till into the clay.

Q. What can you do to make sand hold water?

A. Add everything listed in the previous answer except the sand.

Q. When do you add compost to a garden?

A. In the fall, and let it set on top till spring.

Q. If you spade a garden in the fall, do you have to do it again in the spring?

A. I only spade or roto-till in the fall if I need the

134

exercise, and I do that before I add my compost or other rakings. Then I spade again in the spring; that's a must. Soil becomes compacted (pushed down) from snow and rain, and if you just scuff it up with a rake you don't give the new seed and plants a fair start.

Q. *When is the best time to dig up your garden?*

A. If you have never had a garden in a certain spot before, remove the sod and throw it into your compost pile in the fall. Now add the collection found in answer to the question on breaking up clay and wait till spring to spade in. Never spade, dig, till, or cultivate a garden until soil will crumble in your hand after being squeezed firmly.

Q. *What good do eggshells and coffee grounds do for garden dirt?*

A. I told you once before—soil! It helps to break up heavy soil or clay.

Q. *We have adobe soil. What can we do for it?*

A. The same thing your soil brother did with the problem about breaking up clay.

Q. *How much and when do you add lime to your garden?*

135

A. I have found that you should lime once every three years at a rate of one quart jar per 100 square feet applied in the fall or apply liquid lime in the spring at 2 ounces per 100 square feet.

Q. Should you add fertilizer to the soil before you plant?

A. I add about a pound of garden food per 100 square feet in the fall and then feed my garden with a liquid garden food right after I plant in the spring.

Q. Every year my garden has been carried away by root maggots, cutworms, corn borers, and so on. When, how, and with what can I save my garden?

A. Apply 50 percent Chlordane vegetable powder or Diazinon to the soil in the fall.

Q. How do you build a raised garden?

A. Make a frame out of 2 x 10 timbers, or cement blocks, and fill with good garden soil. A raised garden can be built right on top of clay, cement, a tarred roof—anywhere you can find with full, open sun. It's also a good idea to use a wood preservative available at a paint store to keep the wood from rotting.

Q. What can you grow in a raised garden?

136

A. Anything you can grow in a regular garden if you have the room.

Q. *What grows best in tubs and big planters?*

A. The same as in the preceding answer except that close to the house I kind of like to use my planters for vegetables that we use in salads. They look nice on a patio—parsley, leaf lettuce, swiss chard, spinach.

Q. *Most of my garden is in the sun, but about 25 percent is in some shade. What can grow in the shade?*

A. Beans and cabbage don't do too badly in the shade, but you must watch out for insects a little more in shady spots than in the sun. Bugs like a cool spot on a hot day just the way you and I do.

Q. *How do you plant on the side of a hill?*

A. Very carefully, or your garden will wash away. We call it "contour planting." That means the rows follow around the hill and not up and down. All gardens should have about a 5-degree slope to the southeast.

Q. *What is the best location for a garden?*

A. There is no doubt about it. An open area with no trees to shade it and a 5-degree slope to the south-

137

east is the best. And any other spots that are in full sun are great.

Q. If you have a good spot to grow a garden, but it is very small and you want flowers as well as vegetables and berries, can you plant them all together without altering the flavor of food or fragrance of flowers?

A. Absolutely. I never give it a thought. I use salad greens, spinach, mustard, lettuce, and red cabbage as borders in front of evergreens while growing pole beans up my down spouts near my roses, and I mix carrots and parsnips with marigolds as sidewalk borders.

Q. Do strawberries, raspberries, and blueberries need a different soil and location from my regular garden? Can they really be grown with each other?

A. Heck no, they aren't any different from any other member of the garden team. Yes, they can and should be grown together.

Q. How do you figure how big an area you need for a vegetable garden for the size family you have?

A. The way my Grandma Putt taught me was to add up all the heights of my family and then multiply by the same answer, and that's the number of square feet you need for your home garden. I'm 6 feet, Ilene

138

is 5 feet, Jeff is 5 feet, Pat is 5 feet, Diane is 5 feet, and Kathy is 3 feet—which totals 29 feet. Now 29 feet x 29 feet = 841 square feet. So that's the garden space I would need to provide for fresh, frozen, stored, and dried food for one year for my family.

Q. How many rows or how many plants of each should you plant?

A. You always plant more of the things you like than the things you don't. That stands to reason. But I use this formula as an all-around rule. Row crops (carrots, radishes, parsnips) are planted in length at your height, or a 6-foot row for sons over thirteen years of age and fathers; ½ that length for mothers and daughters over fifteen, ⅓ for any under that age. Tomatoes and peppers should be three plants for dad and one each for all other members.

Q. Do you really have to draw a picture of your garden?

A. No, you don't have to, but it sure does make it easier to remember where you had what this year three years from now when you are rotating your crops. I use a large paper grocery bag cut open and draw with magic markers in color. Then I write notes on it all season. It becomes my garden diary.

Q. Are seeds you send away for as good as the ones you buy in the seed racks in your grocery store?

139

A. No. Whoever started that rumor should have his mouth washed out with soap. I use both sources. The seed men often have a larger and newer selection than the racks, because there may not be a large enough quantity for the packet-seed market yet.

Q. *I have some two-year-old seed. Is it still good?*

A. Test it. Sprinkle five or six seeds on top of a pot of damp soil, cover, and germinate. If it does, it is; if it doesn't, it's not. Better to test it now than wait three or four weeks to see if it comes up in your garden just to find out you lost—time and space.

Q. *Which seeds go in early and how early?*

A. The vegetable and fruit plants I call tough are asparagus, broccoli, Brussels sprouts, cabbage, celery, collards, garlic, kale, kohlrabi, mustard, onion sets (and all other onions), peas, radishes, rhubarb, rutabaga, spinach, strawberries, and turnips. When I say early I mean anywhere between a month or two weeks before the last frost in your area.

Q. *How early can you plant the lettuces?*

A. I will generally gamble and plant lettuce, as well as beets, carrots, cauliflower, endive, parsley, parsnips, potatoes and swiss chard, about a week before the last frost. Then I hold my breath.

140

Q. Is it true that the best time to plant corn is on Memorial Day?

A. That's as good a guide date as any for snow-country planting. You can also add artichoke, beans, cantaloupe, eggplant, okra, peanuts, peppers, pumpkins, squash, tomatoes, and watermelon.

Q. How deep do you plant corn? The birds always seem to get mine.

A. All the large seeds are planted 2 inches deep. Beans and onion sets should be 2 inches as well. Beets, cucumbers, melons, peas, and squash are planted at one inch, while broccoli, Brussels sprouts, cabbage, cauliflower, celery, carrots, eggplant, lettuce, mustard, parsnips, peppers, radishes, spinach, and turnips are happy with a ½-inch soil blanket and tomatoes only want a ¼-inch.

Q. Which seeds are the best to start indoors and when?

A. The truth of the matter is you can start any seed indoors, but as a rule only individual plants, not row crops, are started indoors: broccoli, Brussels sprouts, cabbage, cantaloupe, cauliflower, celery, collards, cucumbers, eggplant, onions, peppers, squash, tomatoes, and watermelon are the most popular. Corn can also be started indoors. You plant most of your seed in individual peat pots or clay pots

141

in a very light planter mix. I use commercial mixes used for African violets and start them in a Gro-Varium (a specially designed tray with a plastic dome and soil-heating cable unit, made by Wrapon Company). I start all my seeds from 6 to 8 weeks before they are to go outside.

Q. Is it true that you should always plant cucumbers on the east side of a garden?

A. As far as I know, it's true, but I carry it a step farther. All vine crops—such as cantaloupe and watermelon, not to mention squash—are planted to the east end of my garden because these plants always grow to the east and run over the top of other plants.

Q. Do you really have to plant so many corn seeds to the mound in order to get corn?

A. Yep! According to my teachers (old experts), 4 seeds to the mound, and if you are planting in rows, plant seed 9 to 12 inches apart and 2 feet between the rows with at least 3 rows. And always plant on the west side of your garden so the corn can protect the other plants from warm, dry winds.

Q. How often should you feed corn?

A. Never use garden food with newly planted seed or it will rot it. I feed the first time when it is a foot high

142

with any lawn food and again when its beard (silk) shows.

Q. *What good does soaking corn seed do?*

A. Improves the odds on its growing in your favor. I soak all vegetable seed in a cup of tea in the refrigerator for 24 hours before I plant. The results are worth the effort and extra day.

Q. *Corn takes up so darn much space for so long a time with little return. Can I grow something along with it?*

A. Sure you can, but be kind to both groups. I interplant pole beans. The beans grow up the stalks and don't hurt a thing.

Q. *If farmers grow pumpkins in corn fields, why can't I?*

A. There is no reason on this earth why you can't, except how many pumpkins can you use? I have found that my corn and cucumbers have become great friends. You see, lots of folks don't know it but corn likes its feet in the shade and top in the sun. So my cucumbers, melons, and squash can be a growing mulch for my corn.

Now that may seem contrary to what I said earlier about only to the east. It's not. I said they would grow over other *small* plants. Corn is not one of them.

143

Q. How often should you cultivate corn?

A. Are you kidding? *Me?* Cultivate corn? That's too much trouble, my friend. Eight or 9 inches of straw or grass clippings down the rows and through the plants does all the cultivating needed.

Q. I just can't seem to get beans to grow for me, because I have such heavy soil. What can I do?

A. First, read the answer near the start of this chapter to the question about breaking up clay. Next, dig a trench 10 inches deep, 5 inches wide, and fill with an equal mixture of sharp sand and peat moss. That will give the beans a good start. Next, drive metal stakes 6 feet tall into the ground and stretch wire between top and bottom. Then, every place you plant a seed, fix an upright wire. This is for pole beans. Bush beans I grow up through a large fruit-juice can with top and bottom out of it.

Q. What do you feed beans?

A. Garden food in the early spring. Beans give more nitrogen back to the earth than they eat.

Q. When do you thin beans?

A. Never. I plant pole beans 2 feet apart and bush beans 9 inches apart.

144

Q. *How do you keep the damn coons, mice, birds, squirrels, or whatever from digging up your beans?*

A. The same way my Grandma Putt cured me from biting my fingernails. She always cleaned out "gourds" by drilling a hole with her potato peeler and saved the seeds for next year. She also saved the juice and filler and added water to it and kept it in a jar. She would put some of this juice on my nails, and the rest she poured on corn and other big seed just as she planted it. Folks, it is the bitterest juice you ever tasted, and I reckon the varmints must hate it as much as I did.

Q. *Why do my lima beans get so leggy and not have many beans?*

A. You must pick them just as quickly as they get mature beans, and they want a sunny, warm location, with good drainage. Very little food is necessary. Beans and peas are the best investment a gardener can make as they give the biggest return for space and time invested.

Q. *I think I have every seed catalog offered, and the more I look at them the more confused I become. Each company says their seeds are new and improved. Which are and which aren't, and which bean would you recommend in each category?*

145

A. I wish to give all the seed growers a pat on the back because they are all working hard to develop varieties that will resist bugs and diseases and need less water, food and care—all for our benefit. So, to answer the first part of your question, they are all improved. Next, in my opinion, top-crop snapbean is a great bush bean, while you just can't seem to beat Kentucky Wonder as a reliable, tasty, heavy producing pole bean, and I always recommend Clark's Green-seeded Bush lima bean.

Q. *Why don't my beets ever get any bigger than a Ping-Pong ball?*

A. The soil is too heavy, probably clay. Beets like light, loose soil. In heavy soil, dig a trench 4 inches wide and 8 inches deep. Fill with ground-up leaves and sawdust; beets need heat, light soil, and sand.

Q. *Can beets be started indoors?*

A. Can they ever! I use my papier-mâché egg cartons (cup part) filled with light house-plant soil and start them in my Gro-Varium, and by the way, my favorite variety is named after my home town, Detroit Dark Red beet.

Q. *I want to grow my beets organically. What kind of food do you recommend?*

146

A. Take your table scraps (not meat or bones), and place them in your blender. Now, add water to fill up your blender and liquefy the scraps. Take this liquid out and pour it on your beets and the rest of your garden, and Watch It Grow!

Q. *What do you feed beets?*

A. Any garden food in the spring.

Q. *What's the earliest and the latest you can plant beets?*

A. The earliest is as soon as you can work the soil, and the latest is around August 15 in the East and Midwest, and July 15 in the North.

Q. *How do you grow broccoli so that the heads don't grow all over the place?*

A. Broccoli, cabbage, cauliflower, and Brussels sprouts are all in the same family, and as a rule take up a hell of a lot of room. So remember that when you plan your garden. They are also planted at the same time and in cooler country from small plants started indoors. As for broccoli, I use Green Comet, because it is early and tight-headed.

Q. *What kind of soil does broccoli like?*

A. It can stand some dampness but not a lot.

147

Q. Can I plant my broccoli, cabbage and Brussels sprouts together?

A. I would, so I can take care of them all the same and watch for the same insects. As a matter of fact, that's an excellent idea. By all means, do it.

Q. How early should you start your Brussels sprouts, cabbage, broccoli, and cauliflower?

A. Because I use my Gro-Varium, I start mine 3 weeks before I am going to set them out. If you don't have a Gro-Varium, start them 5 weeks before.

Q. Can I safely mulch cabbage without inviting insects?

A. As I have stated throughout this book, I mulch my whole damn garden, lock, stock, and barrel, with grass clippings, straw, corn cobs, buckwheat hulls, sawdust, etc., and don't have any more trouble with bugs than anyone who doesn't mulch.

Q. My neighbor said you can use grass fertilizer to feed cabbage! Can you?

A. Your neighbor is right. I use grass food for anything that grows above the ground, except tomatoes.

Q. Why do my carrots always grow all gnarled up, short and fat, or not at all.

148

A. Carrots like rich, light soil 8 to 10 inches deep. If the soil is clay, just dig an 8- to 10-inch wedge and fill with sand, peat, leaves, and sawdust. Your carrots are probably in heavy soil. Carrots don't do well in shade and prefer bright, sunny areas. Carrots are fed with any garden food after foliage appears. I plant my seeds 3 inches apart, one at a time. I would rather do it in the beginning than thin them later.

Q. *Can you really plant cucumbers in hanging baskets?*

A. You want another big surprise? Cucumbers also make great house plants. The only problem with growing them in hanging baskets is that they like cool, slightly damp and shaded areas.

Q. *Should you let cucumbers run on the ground or stake them?*

A. I like to grow them up fences or trellises and mulch their feet.

Q. *Are eggplants hard to grow?*

A. Not as a rule, but what most folks forget is that eggplants never stop eating. Eggplants like rich, light soil and a sunny location. Plant seeds ½ inch deep, 2 feet apart, and 2 feet between rows; feed with liquefied table scraps regularly.

149

Q. When do you know when to eat kohlrabi?

A. That's a super question! Do you know that most folks that have grown it for years don't know the answer! Kohlrabi is part of the cabbage kingdom, but you eat the base, not the foliage or the root, and you eat it as soon as it has formed to the size of a handball or it will be like eating a croquet ball (woody).

Q. What makes lettuce get mushy and slimy?

A. This usually happens when lettuce is planted too late in the spring. Lettuce does not like warm weather, but can be grown in hot weather if grown in light shade. Lettuce is a very shallow-rooted plant that needs plenty of food and must be kept damp.

Q. How come melon seed doesn't sprout as well as other seed?

A. Since they are in a larger case with a soft center, melons are often injured or crushed in handling or shipping. Cantaloupe, pumpkin, watermelon, cucumber, and squash all fall into the same problem area. To avoid disappointment, why don't you soak your seed in a cup of lukewarm tea for 2 hours, then soak a big bath towel (old one) in weak tea, and wring out. Now spread your seed in a row in the middle of the towel and fold the towel over the seed. Place all in a plastic garbage bag and keep at 70 degrees for 6

150

days. Then remove the seed and plant the sprouted seed in the garden.

Q. Why do melons rot on the ground side, or take so long to ripen?

A. Heat speeds up the ripening. Place young melons on a brick while they are still attached to the vine and speed up the ripening.

Q. Can mustard greens be grown indoors?

A. They sure can—in large pots on a sunny windowsill, and they're usually ready to eat in 5 to 6 weeks after the planting. That's the same outside. Remember, you can plant mustard greens early and again in August-September as they like cool weather. For those of you who have never eaten greens, you don't know what you are missing.

Q. How do you get onion sets to be big onions for storing?

A. Onions can be grown from seed or sets, both of which are tough little fellows and can be planted as early as you can get into the garden. Plant early sets or seeds 4 inches apart and let them grow. Eat every other one as you hanker to. Never let the seed pod form on top. Pinch it off. In late August-early September, bend the tops over to stop the top growth.

151

Soon the bulb will get bigger. Pull it up and let it dry in the sun for 2 or 3 weeks and then store.

Q. Is it true that parsnips grow all winter in frozen ground?

A. Well, it's almost true. They don't grow in frozen ground, but you can leave them in the ground all winter and dig them up as you need them. They taste better after a heavy frost. Parsnips grow and like the same soil as their cousins, the carrots. Parsnips are my very favorite vegetable and make super wine.

Q. I heard that you do not have to plant peas in soil, but in straw. Is that true?

A. Sort of. You can sow peas over lightly tilled soil, near a fence or wire (chicken) screen, and cover with 10 to 12 inches of straw, and they grow super! Peas like to grow up something, so give them a hand.

Q. Why don't peppers grown from seed planted right in the garden do well?

A. It's probably due to you, your garden location, and the soil, not the seed. It's true that plants do better than seed, but that's because they are stronger. Peppers like a dry, light soil in a sunny spot, and they will do fine.

152

Q. *I want to grow my own potatoes. Where do I begin?*

A. You can begin by deciding if you want to grow only enough to harvest and eat or to store some as well. Buy good seed potatoes from your garden center in March or April, and plant in good, well-drained soil. You can plant in mounds or on top of the soil with a foot of marsh hay or straw piled on top (my favorite way). Cut seed potatoes in pieces with at least two eyes, plant in April, May, and June 1.

Q. *What plant can't you plant pumpkins near?*

A. Squash! These two plants cross-pollinate when put together, leaving you with some pretty odd-looking offspring.

Q. *Why won't radishes grow well in the middle of summer?*

A. Because they like cool weather. Early spring and late fall are best, but if planted in light shade they will provide a pretty good selection of sizes for eating.

Q. *If you use spinach as a border planting under evergreens, won't it pick up a flavor?*

A. I have never had that problem, and I use it as a border all the time. Spinach loves shade, where it is

153

cool and damp. Feed spinach a little lawn food every 3 weeks.

Q. Can you plant more than one kind of squash on a mound?

A. You sure can. It's only pumpkins and squash that get each other in trouble. I grow zucchini and yellow summer squash back to back in a mound with a clay sewer tile buried ⅓ of its length into the soil so I can water easily. Acorn and butternut are a must for winter squash. So many good squash varieties are available that I try a different one each season. Remember, squash likes sandy, gravelly soil, so make heavy soil light or make foot-high mounds of sandy loam.

Q. When do you start tomato seeds indoors so that they don't get too leggy (tall) and fall over?

A. I start mine 6 weeks before it's time to go outside, in my Gro-Varium. When the new plants are 2½ to 3 inches tall, I plant them in paper cups deeper than they were growing in my Gro-Varium. As a matter of fact, I leave only the top layer of leaves above the soil (use a commercial African violet soil). I let this grow until it is 9 inches high and again transplant, this time into a 4-inch clay pot, not disturbing the soil ball, but planting deeper than it was in the cup.

Q. Is it really necessary to stake tomatoes?

154

A. It is unless you like sore backs and rotten tomatoes. There are lots of ways to keep tomatoes off
the ground without staking. Large-squared old
fence, wooden frames, and plastic pails with top and
bottom cut out do fine. I still like stakes. As soon as I
plant my tomatoes, I drive a 6-foot metal pole only,
and as the plants grow, I tie them up with pieces of
nylon stocking—not rope or twisturns. I use metal
poles because they attract static electricity, and
nylon because it does the same. Makes stronger,
greener plants and deeper fruit.

Q. Do you have to take suckers off tomatoes?

A. No, you don't have to, and most folks don't want to
go to the trouble. I do because I plant fewer plants
and want more fruit. I remove free-loading suckers
that ride along for a free meal and don't produce.

*Q. Can you really get bigger tomatoes faster by set-
ting the blossoms with gibberellic acid?*

A. It's a must. In my garden I use Blossom Set (Science Products) on all my plants to insure maximum
pollination for the most fruit per plant. You try it once
and you'll never be without it.

*Q. What makes the bottoms of my tomatoes turn soft
and grayish black every year?*

A. It's caused by improper distribution of water to

155

the plant. If you will wait until about 4 weeks after you plant your tomatoes, cover the roots with 4 or 5 inches of grass clippings or straw, you should never be bothered by blossom end rot.

Q. What makes tomatoes stop growing in the middle of the summer, the fruit fall off, the leaves curl up, and the plant die?

A. This is called "fusarium wilt" and can be controlled by spraying the soil in the fall and early spring with the fungicide Benomyl. If you had the problem, treat it, 'cause it sure as hell ain't going away by itself.

Q. Is it true that pipe, cigar, and cigarette smoke can ruin a tomato crop?

A. That's the truth, friend. I suggest smokers wash hands well before working in the garden. The disease is called "tobacco mosaic." It also loves potatoes.

Q. Is liquid cow manure good for tomatoes?

A. Only if the cows don't step on the tomatoes! Sure it is, and so is fish fertilizer, garden food, and any of the labeled tomato foods. I use one called Tomato Gro (10–52–17).

Q. Can tomatoes grow in shade?

156

A. Not very well. They like a bright spot in your garden. And there is a bright spot—they don't mind fairly heavy soil.

Q. *We love turnip greens, but they don't do too well in the summer. How come?*

A. 'Cause they don't like hot weather. Plant early in May and again in August. You can have some luck in the summer if you plant in part shade, but don't expect wonders.

Q. *We just don't have any luck with watermelons, and I have tried all kinds. We have good, rich black soil. Why don't they like us?*

A. It's not you; it's your garden location! If you had a light hillside your watermelons would grow to the bottom of the hill before you could get there. Dry soil, in a sunny location, with real good drainage. And don't forget to remove any sick or dried blossoms.

Q. *Is it true that there is a yellow watermelon?*

A. It's true! The meat is red, but the hide turns yellow when it's ripe. It's called Golden Midget; and it is super for growing in small areas in the North. It takes 65 days! Not bad, eh?

Q. *Is it a fact that rhubarb leaves are poison?*

157

A. 'Tis a fact, so don't eat the leaves, but don't let this scare you away from planting some. Plant a root in the spring and don't expect any rhubarb till the following year.

Q. *When do you plant raspberries for best results?*

A. In the spring, in good, well-drained soil, 12 inches apart and 4 feet between rows. Trim the roots some when you plant and then mulch with grass or straw. Feed 3 weeks later with any liquid plant food. I use my Tomato Gro. Every spring after I have fruit, I feed again and cut back to 3 inches off the ground. Move the mulch and look for young shoots. Cut out all but the strongest and will you ever have a garden full of raspberries—big, fat, and sweet. Please grow some.

Q. *How long can I count on my strawberries to produce?*

A. For years and years if you do it right! Plant in the spring, good, healthy fresh plants in good, rich, tilled, light soil. As soon as you can get your tools into the soil, plant 12 inches apart with rows at least 4 feet apart. I use my long-handled bulb planter to make my holes and then spread the roots out over a small stone the size of a golf ball or a ball of soil. Don't plant any deeper than it was at the nursery. Now, feed with your liquid garden food or a good, dry food and pick off any blossoms the first year. Cover with straw in the fall and uncover in the early spring. The main plant

158

will grow babies on runners. Let them go, but don't let them bunch up. Thin out some babies if you have to. At the end of three years, spade the big plants under and let the grown-up kids do their thing, growing babies back over where grandma used to grow. Get good varieties for your area; your nursery man will help you select. Also use Science Berry Set as directed.

Q. What do you use to control the eight jillion bugs that drive me and my garden nuts?

A. I think you just about hit the number on the head; it's a shame we can't do the same to all the bugs. I can list every insect I have been asked about here but both of us would get tired—me of writing, which I do by hand, and you of reading. So let's make it easy on us and hard on the bugs. If they crawl, fly, hop, skitter, slink on, over, or around your garden, use dusts or sprays of Sevin, Zineb, Maneb. Malathion, Methoxychlor, Kelthane, Rotenone, Zineb, and Maneb are for fungus diseases, which are, in fact, airborne bugs as far as I am concerned. As for the creeps that hide in the soil and pick on our poor defenseless plants from below—Chlordane or Diazinon can usually handle the toughest of them.

Q. Are these garden weeders any good, or will they kill my vegetables or hurt my pets or me and my family?

159

A. I swear by them (except that they won't let me swear). They do a great job, and if used in combination with mulch, you should have nothing to do but water, feed, and harvest.

Q. *I want to grow an herb garden. What's the best location?*

A. A location where nothing else likes to grow. Herbs as a rule like sandy, gravelly soil, since most of them are in the same family as many a weed.

Q. *Does an herb garden have to be formal?*

A. Of course not. Where did you ever get that idea? Plant herbs for convenience. Some of the more fragrant ones should be planted close to the house or patio, while dill, the gangly one, is usually hidden. You have probably seen the pictures of a wagon wheel buried in the ground and different herbs planted in the spokes. Let your imagination be your guide.

Q. *Which are the best herbs to plant for the average home?*

A. There is no such place as an average home; each home is special. But for a list of the herbs you might get the most out of, I think I can come up with something. Chives, parsley, dill, thyme, sage, mint, fennel, chervil, borage, basil, anise, rosemary, tarragon, sweet marjoram, savory, and coriander. That ought to keep your home, kitchen, and life spiced up.

160

roses

The rose is by far the most popular flower in the world. In the United States alone over 50 million are sold each year through garden centers and department and grocery stores. About 49 million are destined to die, all needlessly.

Roses are the easiest plant in your garden to care for. The rose is also the most prestigious plant you can have growing. If you can grow roses, folks will be sure that you are an expert in all kinds of gardening. If I had to pick the toughest plant in the garden, I would pick the rose. Right now you are looking out your window at some poor sickly-looking rose bush and saying, "My rose bush, tough? It doesn't look like it could fight its way out of a wet paper bag!" Remember, I did not say they were indestructible, but with a little effort on your part roses will pay their share of the rent faster than any other bloomer you can think of.

Roses want a bright, sunny spot with rich, loose soil and excellent drainage. That's what they want. What they get is heavy clay, plenty of shade, and a hole full of water. Also, seldom are roses fed. What they would like is to be fed a handful of garden food (girl food) once a month, watered from below, and given a soap-and-water shower once a week to discourage insects and disease.

Q. Why don't my roses look like the ones from the florist?

A. Probably because they are not the same class. Cutting roses are hybrid teas which produce one, sometimes two roses per stem, with some fragrance. They have been crossed with the tea rose of China. You can purchase, plant, and harvest hybrid teas in your yard as pretty as theirs.

Q. Can you dis-bud floribundas and come up with a large, long-stem rose?

A. Yeah, but why would you want to go to all that trouble? Just plant tea roses. Floribundas grow their flowers in clusters; the plant is an excellent accent plant, as well as being displayed by itself.

Q. What kind of rose can you use in a rather small

162

rose garden and still get the most color and flowers for house use?

A. Man, oh, man, it's got to be any of the grandifloras. These are really big mamas, with color galore and big flowers—and they are strong as hell.

Q. What's the best type of rose for New Mexico and Arizona?

A. What you should have said is hot, arid areas, and I would say polyanthas. By the way, they grow darn near everywhere. The flowers are a big cluster of smaller flowers that make great centerpieces.

Q. Are tree roses tough to take care of?

A. I don't think so, if you will just remember to protect the graft (knot) at the top. I use newspaper and tape, plus straw. Some folks bend them over and bury them. I find that, more often than not, the darn trunk breaks.

Q. I would like to know the name of an everblooming climber that really does bloom all season, and not just once.

A. If any climber is properly planted in good, rich light soil, fed once a month with a rose or garden food, and is in bright sun and watered well, it will bloom all season. Also, it's just as important to cut the

163

spent flowers from a climber as it is from any other type of rose. Climbing Show Garden is far and away the best climber. She is pink. Improved Blaze, Amethyst Rose, and Gladiator are my choices.

Q. *Can you really grow roses in a rock garden?*

A. You sure can and, boy, do they ever look great. I suggest that you use any of the climbing floribundas. You can use climbers to cascade down a wall as well.

Q. *My neighbor only buys her roses by mail from Jackson & Perkins, Armstrong, or Star. She says they have better roses than you can buy in stores. Is this true?*

A. Those just happen to be three of the most reputable mail-order houses in the world, so she can't go too far wrong. But you can buy top-quality roses from local merchants as well. I find that newer varieties are available sooner through the mail-order houses. I buy from both.

Q. *Are bare-root roses safe to buy? They're cheaper.*

A. Yes, they're safe to buy, but they are not always cheaper. When roses are harvested, they are pulled from the ground, soil taken from the roots and stored in cool, damp cellars in the fall. They are then shipped to your nurseryman and mail-order houses bare-root. Mail-order houses then put straw or shavings around the roots, slip on a plastic bag to keep the roots damp, and send them to you. Your nurseryman pots his in plantable containers and grows them to sell you started roses. If you can buy "bareroot," you save handling charges.

Q. Are potted roses better than packaged roses?

A. No, but they're more expensive. With potted roses, you can plant instant flowers at any time of the season.

Q. Should you buy packaged roses with lots of growth or none?

A. None, if at all possible. Don't select packaged roses with any lengths of growth, just little breaks. After all, you are going to cut two-thirds of the top off before planting, just above an outside break. New growth saps the strength of your new bush if it is not in the ground.

Q. Why do they put wax on the canes of rose bushes? The ones I buy this way seem to die more often than ones that aren't waxed.

A. Canes are waxed to keep moisture in the wood. I don't like to buy waxed canes if I can help it, but if I must, I pull the wax away from all the little breaks (buds).

165

Q. I like to order my roses early because I get a better selection. How early can I purchase and safely store them?

A. If you have room to store them at between 35 and 40 degrees, you can order at any time.

Q. Solve an argument. My wife says you should buy skinny rose bushes and I say big, fat ones! Who is right?

A. Bow to the lady, she's right. Purchase roses with canes the size of a pencil. I'll tell you a secret. Most nontrained garden salespeople and management think these are runts and mark them down, so I waltz in and do them (Ha!) a favor and take them off their hands.

Q. Why do you have to cut new roses back so far?

A. To give them a better than halfway chance to get a good start. The less top growth the newly planted roots have to supply food to, the better chance of quick rooting.

Q. When is the better time to plant roses, fall or spring?

A. I plant most of my roses around September 15 and cover them with a mix of leaves and soil. I also

166

Q. When do you prune climbing roses?

A. Suckers should be pruned out at any time; prune other growth in the early spring when new growth appears, same as the rest.

Q. Why don't you have to mulch climbers?

A. I always mulch my root stock and shield my climbers from a southwest wind with burlap.

Q. Why can't you use plastic garbage bags to mulch roses?

A. Because the roses can't breathe, silly! I'm just kidding. Roses must go dormant, asleep. When you put a plastic bag over the top and the sun comes out, it gets warm in the bag and wakes up the rose and sap begins to flow. The sun goes behind a cloud, and it gets freezing inside and kills the rose. Need any more reason for not using plastic bags?

Q. When do you mulch roses?

A. When they get cold. I wait till the temperature goes below freezing.

Q. If your roses were small and the leaves yellow last season, what's wrong?

169

A. The plant was probably starving to death. Feed every 3 or 4 weeks, up until August 15.

Q. *Should you dormant-spray in the spring as well as in the fall?*

A. And how! Dormant-spray with Volk oil and lime sulphur in the fall before you mulch, and then again in the spring.

Q. *When is the best time to move a rose bush?*

A. I like to move them in September if at all possible, or as early in the spring as I can get a shovel in the soil. Always water right after you move older plants, and fill them up for a week or two if you move them in the spring. As a matter of fact, you can mulch them for three weeks just as you would for winter.

Q. *What's the best mulch for roses?*

A. I just can't see wasting anything that's worth using, so I find ground-up leaves are the best. I rake my leaves into a row, put the grass catcher on my mower, and mow the leaves. It grinds them up fine. Then I use them mixed with a little soil to hold them down, or put a chicken-wire basket around them half filled with the leaves.

Q. *Can soil wear out from roses?*

170

A. It's not the roses that cause it. It's just lack of attention. In the spring add ½ cup of Epsom salts per 4 square feet; add bone meal in the fall.

Q. *What's the best way to water roses?*

A. Always let the water trickle out and flood the soil. I also cut the ends out of large juice cans and bury them between my roses and fill them with small stones. I then water and feed into the can. This way the water goes deep and so does the food, which makes my roses develop deep roots that protect them from hot, dry days.

Q. *Can you mulch under your roses?*

A. Absolutely! Saves work and roses. I use tar paper and cover with decorative bark or stone.

Q. *Why do they say the more you cut roses, the more you get?*

A. If you cut in the right spot you force the rose to throw another flowering spur. The right spot is just above a 5-leaf cluster. If you cut wrong, the rose has to grow another stem and then throw a flower spur for a 5-leaf, so you see it takes longer. Also, the flower that is fading is still taking food for a "hip" seed pod—which is a waste of food unless you use the hips for tea, jam, or soup.

171

Q. *What's all this foolishness about outside eyes?*

A. It's not foolishness. It's honest injuns! To have healthy, full roses you must keep the center open, which means forcing the foliage to grow away from the center. This is accomplished by cutting just above an outside bud in the spring and above an outside 5-leaf cluster when cutting and pruning roses for bouquets or spent blooms.

Q. *Should you cultivate under roses?*

A. If you don't use a mulch, it's a good idea to work the soil up from time to time.

Q. *Which is best, wood or aluminum trellises?*

A. I prefer metal supports for all plants because of the added benefit of static electricity; but wood ones, cedar or redwood, are fine.

Q. *Does it hurt to plant other flowers with roses?*

A. I don't mind—nor does the rose as long as it's not bulbs. That's just not fair to either one.

Q. *My leaves are never really dark green. They are sort of pale and the ribs are greener. What's wrong?*

A. That's an iron deficiency and can be remedied with Green-Gard Micronized Iron in the spring.

172

Q. Can you take a cutting from a rose and get a plant?

A. Right-o. You can take a summer cutting. Summer cuttings are young branches 8 inches long. Remove all the leaves except the top two, bury half of the stem in a bright, sunny, well-drained location, and cover with a mason jar. When new growth appears, remove the jar.

Q. How do you layer a rose bush?

A. Pull a one-year-old cane down so it touches the soil. Now, dig a shallow pocket 2 inches deep and place the cane in the pocket. Pin it down, cover with soil leaving 6 to 8 inches of the bud above the ground, and place a brick on top of the soil to keep it down. When it roots, cut it off and plant it where you want it.

Q. Can you really eat rose petals?

A. I love them in tossed salad with Italian dressing. Yes, you can eat them. The light colors are best. Like eating lettuce, break off the heavy base of the petal and only eat the tender part. They really dress up salads.

Q. Why do the leaves curl up on my roses?

A. Probably because you have a visitor called a leaf

173

roller. He's a small green worm that ties leaves together and rolls them up while he eats. Spray with Malathion or rose and flower dust made into a spray.

Q. Why don't my rose buds open?

A. Look for a little, hairy bug called a thrip. He punches a hole in the buds. To stop him, dust often with rose dust.

Q. Does planting garlic by roses keep aphids away?

A. Does a pretty darn good job, and a bath with soap and water and Malathion really insures control.

Q. We have rose chafers by the hundred every summer. What can we do?

A. Sprinkle paradichlorobenzene moth crystals on the soil by your roses in early May, and dust in June.

Q. We had scale on our vines climbing up the house, and now I find it on my roses. I didn't know it ate roses.

A. It sure does. Dormant-spray fall and spring with Volk oil.

Q. Isn't any plant sacred from the red spider mite?

A. Not among the roses. Give him a shot of Malathion spray.

174

Q. I am ready to get out of the rose business. Black spot is going to drive my roses to an early grave. What can I do?

A. First, feed your roses regularly, wash with soap and water, and spray with Benomyl fungicide.

Q. What causes roses to get rusty leaves?

A. Not enough sunshine. Usually shaded roses get that way.

Q. How do you keep cane borers out of your roses?

A. Seal any cut you make with pruning paint or nail polish.

Q. My poor rose is infected with mildew. What can I do for her?

A. You can make her life a lot healthier with an application of Benomyl fungicide.

Q. What is the best kind of sprayer to use on roses?

A. I have the Hudson cordless electric sprayer that I think is the best money can buy for my garden. I also use a Hudson compression sprayer with an adjustable nozzle because it puts the spray right where my roses need it.

evergreens

The homeowner of today is no longer referred to as a home gardener. Instead, he is known as a home "yardener." With the exodus to the suburbs, where lots are much larger, we have developed larger yards and smaller gardens. Thus, yardeners instead of gardeners.

With the increased size of property came the necessity to landscape more area. It was inevitable that evergreens, which were found in the woods or on large estates, should become popular. For a number of years in the early 1950s, the demand was greater than the supply. There were neither enough plants nor enough commercial growers. Also, garden centers as we know them today had not yet been developed. By the late 1950s, it seemed that the industry

176

had things under control. The quantity, quality, and assortment were pretty good. The prices were still quite high for the average home yardener and the sizes of the plants were more suited to the professional than the beginner. In the early 1960s the industry got another poke in the ribs. The mass merchandiser discount house was born, and commercial garden people saw the need for and profit in the sale of landscape materials for new homeowners at a reasonable price and in a container they could handle. This is when the container-grown or potted evergreens began to appear. Today landscape nursery stock (evergreens) are available in several types of containers. Sold by many types of outlets, with almost unlimited prices and varieties, evergreens are the most popular planting material in this country today. It does my heart good to see a family out landscaping their own property because they will appreciate each plant more, and the overall plan will reflect the whole family's personality. As a rule, evergreens are hardy guys that don't want much pampering; but they do need some annual care and attention. Evergreens seem to adapt to any kind of soil, but can't survive in a great deal of water. If you will just remember to find out how high and how wide your selection grows and about how long it takes to grow, put it in well-drained soil, feed it at least once a season, spray it in spring, summer, and fall, you can pretty well count on your evergreens keeping you and your family company till old age sets in.

177

Q. *Is it better to plant evergreens balled and bur-laped or in containers?*

A. I just don't think you can beat the results of a well-balled evergreen, but then they are as a rule much larger plants and would almost be impractical to put into containers. Metal cans (the container that the plants are grown in, mostly in California and Oklahoma) are dangerous for planter, not the planted. In most cases the can is cut open or split at the nursery before you leave. Some of the roots may dry out on the way home, or the soil may come loose. I really would prefer the plantable container (papier-mâché) for smaller stock.

Q. *If you have a large number of evergreens to plant, when is the best time?*

A. It doesn't matter how many you have. The best time to plant evergreens is when the days are warm and evenings are cool. That goes for any part of the country.

Q. *Won't bare-root evergreens die?*

A. Yes, if they aren't kept damp and planted prop-erly, which means in a good, comfortable hole.

Q. *We've got the world's hardest clay. Evergreens just don't have a chance. What can I do?*

178

A. You can mound-plant. For this I prefer you purchase evergreens that are balled and burlaped. I have a friend who is a landscape architect who brags he has never lost an evergreen. The trouble with the brag is that he never plants them in the ground, always above. He mound-plants. He places hills of good soil in strategic locations that blend into the contour of the building and then plants the evergreens in the mound. You can do the same thing on your hard clay and not lose a plant, and you can create some pretty original and spectacular designs and effects. Mound-planting can be carried out with all types of plants. When using this style of construction, you must remember to be constantly aware of your permanent grade and leave paths for the water to shed off and away.

Q. Will all broad-leafed evergreens grow in the North?

A. With very few exceptions, yes. But in really cold, blowy areas you must remember to protect them from constant winds. This can be done with burlap screens or snow fence columns with burlap tacked to the front. I gently but firmly tie my azaleas and rhododendrons with an old nylon stocking to keep ice and snow from breaking them.

Q. If you were going to use evergreens as a wind barrier, which would you use—pine, fir, or spruce?

179

A. I would go with pine because they are much faster growing and generally less expensive. Spruce is a rather stodgy guy, handsome, yes, but he can be hard to get along with from time to time, and fir only likes it where it's cool and damp. We usually use either of these last two as a point of "view."

Q. *Can any of the spruces take salt air and still look good?*

A. I'd book odds on a green guy called Dragon Spruce, even though he grows only about half as high as his cousins. Dragon will usually be 60 to 75 feet high and thick.

Q. *What's the fastest-growing spruce?*

A. A burly guy from Norway grows like hell when he is young and handsome, but goes to seed as he gets older. You're usually sorry you planted him when he gets old and scraggly.

Q. *Which is the really pretty silver green spruce?*

A. Koster's Blue, a fine gent you will be glad you asked to stick around.

Q. *What's the showiest of the firs?*

A. I have to cast my vote for Concolor. His Latin name is *Abies concolor.*

180

Q. When I was in California I saw an evergreen, a cypress called Golden Coat. Can I grow it in Fort Wayne, Indiana?

A. The real name is, get this, *Chamaecyparis pisifera Filifera aurea,* or Gold-thread cypress, and, yes, it will do fine. Most folks who are not familiar with this golden yellow evergreen and its brother, Plume cypress, always think they look as if they are about to croak. I think this is as good a place as any to suggest you go to the library and check out a horticultural plate book (color pictures of most plants available for sale in this country). You can then see for yourself if you like the plant's looks.

Q. What's the best wind, sound, and privacy evergreen screen for a swimming pool, one that won't drop needles all over and will stand pool water?

A. Now don't think I am plugging my own product because this plant was not named after me. Baker's Arbovita is probably the best, although Dark Green American is equal to it. I am using both and for the same purpose as you.

Q. What's the willowy evergreen they use for hedges?

A. Ah, heck, that's got to be Canadian or American hemlock. They are both great. They are terrific for shady and/or wet areas as well.

181

Q. *Can arborvitae be pruned and shaped?*

A. They sure can. Early spring will be fine. Use sharp trimmers.

Q. *Are all evergreens fed with the same fertilizer?*

A. I don't know why not. I use any lawn food at a rate of ½ pound per foot of heights and never feed after July 15 in areas where the temperature goes below freezing or it will stimulate new growth which Jack Frost will paint right out of next season.

Q. *What do you feed azalea?*

A. It's a girl, so I feed it with garden food. And you can add ½ pound of coffee grounds each spring per bush and one cup of Epsom salts. Same goes for rhododendron.

Q. *When do you prune azaleas and rhododendrons?*

A. Right after they are done blooming and every three years will really make an improvement.

Q. *Is it true that you have to pull the flowers off both azaleas and rhododendrons?*

A. That's what I was taught, have always done, and will always do. I just don't want to take a chance with those beauties.

182

Q. *When do you prune pines?*

A. When the candles are growing lickety-split. Same with all the evergreens that bear cones. That means in the early summer. Most folks are afraid to prune and do more harm by not pruning than by doing it.

Q. *Of the juniper family, which ones are the easiest to maintain and keep low?*

A. If you mean spreading junipers, I would make the Andorra juniper my first choice. And the winter color is a pretty purple. They take quite a bit of dampness and can be sheared into some lovely ground contours.

Q. *What do you suggest for an upright juniper that doesn't take a lot of work to keep it looking good?*

A. I was afraid no one would ask. Rocky Mountain juniper grows to about 12 feet and is one splendid-looking evergreen.

Q. *What's the lowest-growing evergreen for a rock garden?*

A. The one I would pick would be Tamarix. Its winter color is also purple.

Q. *Why do Japanese yews die so much easier than other evergreens?*

183

A. That's just not so. The yew family is probably the easiest to take care of. They love moderately sandy loam, but most folks put them in heavy black soil. They don't mind a little shade, and if sheared and shaped in early July and sprayed regularly, they are your best investment.

Q. *Do you recommend mulching broad-leafed evergreens?*

A. I do it myself and so do some of the most successful landscapers and gardeners. I use straw at the base of my rhododendrons and azaleas. I screen my holly and ilex.

Q. *What are the names of some good broadleaf evergreens?*

A. Here are the ones you probably won't have any problems finding. Japanese holly (ilex), American holly, mahonia (Oregon grape), boxwood, Pieris Japonica, winter-creeper, rhododendrons and azaleas, mountain laurel, and pyracantha.

Q. *Can evergreens and broadleafs be planted together?*

A. The real name for evergreens as a group is conifers, and the answer is yes. Evergreens are the protectors of the broads.

184

Q. How can you keep dogs from lifting their legs on your evergreens?

A. Hang small pieces of rope that have been dipped in Black Leaf 40. And yell "Shoo" as loud as you can.

Q. Why do moles live under my evergreens?

A. Because they have found a storehouse of food (grubs) that will kill your evergreens. Treat the soil with Chlordane or Diazinon.

Q. What makes the backs of evergreens die, but not the front?

A. Lack of sunshine and dry, hot air coming off the buildings. I spray two times a year with Wilt-Pruf. It's an anti-desiccant, holds moisture in. Spray in the early summer and late fall.

Q. What's the best control for red spider?

A. You just can't beat Kelthane. It's the best miticide we know. Red spider kills more evergreens each year than any other problem.

Q. How do you get rid of bagworms?

A. When I was a kid in Missouri we had to pull them off. Now we spray with Methoxychlor.

185

Q. Can you and/or should you dormant-spray evergreens?

A. I can't think of a better way to make your evergreens like you. Use a para-sealicide as directed. It's packaged by Pratts.

Q. What part of the evergreen do you use for cuttings?

A. New growth that has firmed up. You pull side growth off with a heel (small piece of bark) and place in damp, sharp sand until it roots.

Q. Is it necessary to water evergreens with a root feeder?

A. I don't. I just use my garden hose and let it trickle water for an hour or so.

Q. What's a good preventative spray for all evergreens?

A. I use one teaspoon of liquid dish soap and Malathion as recommended per quart. I spray once a month, using a compression sprayer with an adjustable nozzle so I can get the spray inside where the bugs hide.

Q. How do you keep mice from killing your evergreens?

A. There are several good mice baits available. Use them.

Q. *My upright evergreens break open every winter. What can I do?*

A. The same thing I do. Tie them shoulder, waist, and knee high with old nylon stockings. I tie junipers, arborvitae, and yews as well.

Q. *Can you use wood chips under evergreens as a mulch?*

A. They're as good as anything I can think of, but you had best sprinkle a handful of fertilizer to start them to break down.

Q. *Does it hurt to put a steel or aluminum edging, pounded into the ground, around an evergreen?*

A. Heck, no. We hope the roots aren't that shallow anyhow.

Q. *How and when do you root-prune evergreens?*

A. With a shovel and in the early fall. Take and plunge a spade down into the earth in a circle out at the tips of the lowest branches. Root-pruning is like cutting your toenails. Make darn sure you use a razor-sharp spade.

187

Q. *When and why do you feed evergreens with gypsum?*

A. When is in the fall. I use 5 pounds of gypsum (calcium and sulphur) per plant. Calcium is for roots and the soil, and sulphur is going to give a bug or two a stomachache.

Q. *What do you do to stop spruce galls?*

A. Spray your trees regularly with Malathion and soap and water. If you notice just one or two, cut them off.

Q. *When should you transplant evergreens?*

A. Fall is just the best darn time I can think of.

Q. *Can you use weed killers under or around evergreens?*

A. The so-called garden weeders you can, but as for weed and feeds, I stay away from the weep line of all trees, shrubs, and evergreens. As for liquid weed killers, be awfully careful. They will ruin the foliage for life.

Q. *Can a live Christmas tree be kept alive?*

A. Why, certainly. Keep its foliage moist, ball wet, and after Christmas set it in the garage to let it go dormant gradually, letting the ball freeze. Then plant it in a pre-dug hole.

188

Q. Is it true that it's better to cut a Christmas tree when the weather is warm than a few days before Christmas?

A. It is true you should cut a tree when it still has its sap. I use Prolong tree extender for mine. It's an I.V. of glucose, just like you and I might get.

Q. Can ground up Christmas trees, needles and all, be used as a mulch?

A. It's a lifesaver, but remember it will tend to make the soil acid. If you use this material, add some lime in the spring.

Q. Can you use sanitation-fill sludge to feed evergreens?

A. I have been asked that same question about the areas of the garden. Yes, you can use it and be glad. It's generally free.

Q. I have seen some of the most beautiful designs cut from evergreens. Does this hurt them, and can I do it?

A. You can do it. It's called "topiary"—the shaping of evergreens into forms resembling animals, flowers, buildings, and so on. Rudolph Valentino, the film lover, came to this country as a topiarian.

189

shrubs, hedges, and ground covers

The unsung heroes of the garden world just have to be the flowering shrubs and hedges. For years, this was about all your grandparents had to work with to make their surroundings pleasant. Honeysuckle, spirea, and snowball bushes abounded by the millions, while lilacs were the talk of every town in the spring. With the increased popularity of evergreens, flowering trees, and the flowering broadleafs, the old garden stars, the flowering shrubs, were given lesser parts in the garden show. Then along came the recession of the early 1960s, money was short and space long and shrubs cheap, so out of retirement

190

came the old beauties. The fast-growing forsythia, flowering quince, and mock orange replaced the spirea sewing circle, and for a couple of years, they were in the limelight again. Every dime store, grocery, discount, and garden shop had packaged flower shrubs for sale. But their popularity dipped again. Then came the financial squeeze of the early 1970s and—you guessed it—happy days were here again for the flowering shrubs, hedges, and vines.

I really have to chuckle. When money is available, Cadillacs and Lincolns are a necessity, not a luxury. Well, it seems we feel the same about evergreens. But let the mighty buck stop, and Fords or Chevys will fill the bill. And the same holds true for flowering shrubs.

Honest to gosh, folks, they were always the best buy, best show, and easiest-to-take-care-of addition to anyone's landscape. But I guess it's like everything else in our lives, if it is expensive it must be good.

Now, let's use a little of that common sense and save the dollars and cents and have the best-looking landscape plan on the block for the least amount of money and least amount of care. This group of plants will grow in virtually any kind of soil—with not a whole lot of insect trouble and trimming once a year to keep them happy and showy. Feed the ones with flowers garden food and the ones with foliage lawn food each spring, and you will have a superstar garden, not just another pretty face in the blooming world.

191

Q. *I ordered about $100 worth of flowering shrubs through the mail, and they came in February. What am I going to do? I can't get into the ground yet.*

A. Open the boxes and get a half bale of straw. Carry the open boxes outside, cover them with straw, and then leave them alone. Let it snow, rain, or whatnot. In April take the shrubs out and plant them. They will be just fine. Those ladies of the garden are tough old broads. If you had been kicked around as much as they had, you could take it, too.

Q. *When is the best time to plant flowering shrubs?*

A. Any time you can get a shovel into the ground: early spring, early fall for bare root, spring, summer, fall or even winter for paper container and balled and burlaped. Make darn sure you mulch underneath with wood chips or ground leaves when you plant shrubs.

Q. *Why are flowering shrubs so inexpensive? There must be something wrong with them.*

A. They are so easy to propagate and grow, and they grow so fast that the growers can turn the space more often so the price is less.

Q. *Which kind of shrubs can I use in clay soil?*

A. I can't think of any of them that won't do well in any

soil as long as it's well drained. If you are afraid of trouble, why not mound-plant? That's planting above the normal grade in mounds or hills that blend with the terrain.

Q. What's the best-size plant to put into the landscape plan?

A. Since you can usually buy a much larger plant for less money when it comes to shrubs, why not go for the biggest you can afford so you don't have to wait so long?

Q. Which are the fast-growing shrubs?

A. All of them. Shrubs usually double their size each year. If you don't pay attention, pretty soon you have a mess on your hands.

Q. When planting hedges and shrubs, should you cut all of them back?

A. Before planting, I cut one-third of the foliage back on any shrub or hedge. It gets it off to a better start.

Q. Should newly planted shrubs be dormant-sprayed?

A. Don't ever let me catch you not doing it. Dormant-spray new, old, and middle-aged shrubs in fall and spring.

193

Q. *What are the names of some good vines for trellises and a stone wall?*

A. These are the ones I like: Boston ivy, bittersweet, English ivy, Baltic ivy, clematis, Japanese honeysuckle, *Lantata montevidensis,* wisteria, *Euonymus vegetus.* I want you to understand a thing or so. Vines on buildings are a pain in the you-know-what after a while. They are a ladder for bugs, a nesting place for birds, and make a mess of brick, stone, and wood. They must be sprayed at least every three weeks.

Q. *Is myrtle a weed-free ground cover?*

A. No ground cover is weed-free, but don't let that discourage you from planting it. Ground covers are a godsend in problem places, or where you have large areas to cover, or need a tie-in from bed to bed. If you will plant through holes in tar paper, you can be pretty sure you won't have too many weeds show up.

Q. *What are some ground covers that have flowers as well as good foliage?*

A. Let's start with myrtle, fleece flower, sedum, or dwarf lace plant, bugleweed, and mahonia. Be sure to use a soil cover. Tar paper will do. Bait for mice and spray as a precaution.

Q. *Some information, please, on ground covers with attractive foliage.*

194

A. Purple-leaf winter-creeper is a good start. Pachysandra, Baltic ivy, ajuga (bronze), and cotoneaster.

Q. When and how close do you plant ground covers to get the best growth?

A. I really like to plant my ground covers in September. Perennials are planted about 3 to 4 feet apart, but if you're like me and want quick action, plant them 18 inches to 2 feet. Woody ground covers are planted about 3 feet, and I feed them really early in the spring.

Q. There must be some way to kill slugs and snails in my funkia?

A. I've got the solution to that one. It's a chemical that Dow Chemical developed called Zectran. It's good to use anywhere that slugs are a problem except in a vegetable garden.

Q. What do you think of crown vetch as a ground cover?

A. I used to like it, but man, oh man, that lady runs wild and is more trouble than she's worth.

Q. I would like low hedges other than barberry.

A. Try golden vicary, cotoneaster, St.-John's-wort,

195

Arctic willow, Lodense privet, dwarf privet, and germander. Any should do well. By the way, I love dwarf red barberry. Well, like they say, "Different strokes for different folks."

Q. When you plant hedgerows, how close do you plant them?

A. Hey! Don't forget that the plants you use for hedges can also be used by themselves. So find out how big and wide they grow. As for depth, I plant them so that the crotch is under ground. Be sure to cut back one-third of the foliage. I also plant in the early fall.

Q. We can't use fences in our subdivision (i.e., wire, wood, brick, or stone). But I can use shrubs. What's the best-looking one?

A. In the South and some parts of the West, I go for cherry laurel, English laurel, and aleaster; in the North Chinese elm, honeysuckle, old-fashioned spirea, forsythia, flowering quince, and Canadian hemlock.

Q. When do you prune flowering shrubs?

A. Right after they have bloomed. Remember, they make next year's flowers on this year's wood.

196

Q. *Why don't my hydrangeas bloom?*

A. Probably because you are pruning them in the fall, have them in too much shade, and don't feed them.

Q. *What would keep a lilac from blooming?*

A. The same answer as above and add to it, root-prune in early fall.

Q. *How do you change the color of hydrangeas?*

A. Apply aluminum sulphate to the soil in the fall. My two favorites are Pee Gee for the North and Japanese hydrangea for the South. Oak leaf is another good one for most of the country.

Q. *What makes lilac leaves get rusty in late summer?*

A. Mostly not enough sun. You can use dusting sulphur for this.

Q. *Which lilac has the most smell?*

A. I just love the smell of lilacs in the spring and have never paid that much attention to the differences. The three most common types are Persian, French, and Chinese. I love them all.

197

Q. When is the best time to prune lilacs?

A. Right at the time they are in bloom. The more bouquets you cut, the better for your plants. I got through the fourth grade by taking Grandma Putt's lilac bouquets every day they were in bloom. Lilacs are great to place in a bucket and set in fruit trees to attract more bees.

Q. When do you plant lilacs? And will you get blooms the first year?

A. I just have to say early fall again, and not as a rule will you get flowers because you cut one-third of the wood off and that's got the flowers.

Q. I love flowering almond; is it hardy?

A. You betcha. And as pretty a lady as you will find. Pink, soft flowers bloom in late April and May.

Q. Is tamarix a tree or a bush, and is it considered a weed?

A. Not in my book. It's a great-looking tree/bush with good-looking pinkish red flowers.

Q. What's a good-looking shrub for a damp spot?

A. Any of the dogwoods (shrubs). Red twig varie-

198

gated, Bailey's, or yellow twig will fill the bill, and you will be happy as hell. Hydrangeas aren't bad either.

Q. What's the latest flowering shrub?

A. Yankee hibiscus or, as you know it, Althea Rose of Sharon. Blooms in August and September and sometimes into October. Witch hazel and chasletier come in about that time, too.

Q. Could you have flowers in your yard from January to January in Ohio?

A. And Illinois, Michigan, southern Wisconsin, and Pennsylvania. Not quite year round but darn near. Between bulbs, perennials, and flowering shrubs, March to September, you could go to Thanksgiving. And that ain't too bad, would you say?

Q. What's the best control for borers in lilacs?

A. And other things. I apply paradichlorobenzene moth crystals to the soil in September and April.

Q. What's the best spray for most flowering shrubs?

A. Just use a Malathion and Methoxychlor spray as directed, and you will keep them on the run.

Q. How do you control beetle grubs around shrubs?

199

A. Chlordane, Diazinon.

Q. *How can we stop the Japanese beetle?*

A. With Methoxychlor as directed. You have to remember, though, that the way you spray does make a difference. Make sure that you spray top and bottom of leaves and all of the stem area.

Q. *Do you have to protect ground covers for winter?*

A. I do my perennials with a light cover of straw.

Q. *Can you use the garden weeder in ground cover?*

A. Yep; follow the directions and save a lot of worry and work.

Q. *What's shadblow used for?*

A. This shrub has so many names, it's funny. Amy's chair, poor-man's holly. Its Latin name is *Amelanchier stolonifera*. This plant is used usually in groups of three to get the natural look and, boy, it is lovely-looking. The plant has flowers and berries.

Q. *Which is the churchman's shrub?*

A. Pink-flowering cardinal. Must be a Catholic plant. Why not? Plants are like people. And besides that, it was christened in Latin (*Weigela florida rosea*), as

200

were all the other plants. It flowers like heck in June, and the bees make a line to it. (Get it? Beeline?)

Q. *Can I plant deutzie in Tennessee?*

A. Yes, ma'am! And you will be glad you did—pink and white flowered. Does fine in all but the really cold states and really hot ones.

Q. *Which are shrubs to attract birds?*

A. Snowberry, high bush cranberry, coralberry, and barberry.

Q. *What's good for sandy, dry soil? I would like flowering shrubs.*

A. Privet hedge, forsythia, air pink spirea.

Q. *Are lilies of the valley poisonous?*

A. Yes, but then I never saw Euell Gibbons use them in a recipe.

Q. *Why can't you find hens and chicks anymore?*

A. You just aren't looking in the right places, but if you want its twin sister, try houseleek. Looks like, acts like, and grows like hens, and is available wherever ground covers are sold.

201

Q. My wife won't let me plant honeysuckle because she says it will tear down our fence. Is that true?

A. If your fence is not cross-braced with a metal pole at the top, you will be in a lot of trouble with your wife, like I was with mine for the same reason. It's not worth the aggravation (from your wife).

Q. What's the name of the honeysuckle that looks like an orchid?

A. They all do. That's why they are often called mock orchids. The closest one is Red Gold honeysuckle. Hey, folks, by the way, you just can't beat honeysuckle, even if your wife does get mad at you.

Q. Was my nurseryman kidding when he said there was a dirty word—funkia?

A. You just wrote it. Its real name is *Hosta,* variegated and standard. Take your nurseryman a bar of soap and tell him I said brush his teeth with it. Shame, shame.

Q. What do hookers honeysuckle look like?

A. They are all hookers. They want a free ride—Halls, Golden Flame, and Red Gold. You guys from New Jersey are bad, bad, bad.

Q. Can you prune wisteria?

202

A. Sure you can. When it is in bloom, pruning will do it good.

Q. *Is there a polarios hydrangea that smells good?*

A. You spell as badly as I do. It's called *Hydrangea petiolaris,* or climbing hydrangea, and it smells great. As a matter of fact, it's a real turn-on.

Q. *Should I use lime around shrubs as a regular part of my feeding program?*

A. It's not what they tell you to do, but I go ahead and use lime every spring, only ½ pound or so per bush. Oh! Lime is not food; it's sort of the Alka-Seltzer of the garden world.

Q. *Can pussy willows grow in a wet spot?*

A. Not on your life. *Salix discolor* likes full sun and well-drained soil. It is the best for indoor forcing, but then almost any flowering shrub can be forced to bloom indoors. Try it, along with fruit-tree branches.

Q. *Can gardenias be grown outside as flowering shrubs?*

A. They sure can, in pots or tubs—and they are really worth it.

203